# A Fine Line

## Techniques and Inspirations
## for Creating the Quilting Design

**Melody Crust and Heather Waldron Tewell**

*Photography by
Charles Crust*

**The Quilt Digest Press**
A Division of The McGraw·Hill Companies

**Library of Congress Cataloging-in-Publication Data**

Crust, Melody.
    A fine line : techniques and inspirations for creating the quilting design /
Melody Crust and Heather Waldron Tewell ; photographs by Charles Crust.
       p.   cm.
    Includes bibliographical references.
    ISBN 0-8092-9884-8
    1. Quilting.    2. Quilts—Design.    I. Tewell, Heather Waldron.    II. Title.

TT835.C78    2001
746.46′041—dc21                          2001019369

## *The Quilt Digest Press*
*A Division of The* **McGraw·Hill** *Companies*

1 2 3 4 5 6 7 8 9 0   SSI/SSI   0 9 8 7 6 5 4 3 2 1

ISBN 0-8092-9884-8

This book was set in Minion by Hespenheide Design.
Printed and bound in Singapore by Star Standard Industries.

Drawings by Kandy Petersen
Photography copyright © Charles Crust

McGraw-Hill books are available at special quantity discounts to use as premiums and
sales promotions, or for use in corporate training programs. For more information, please
write to the Director of Special Sales, Professional Publishing, McGraw-Hill, Two Penn
Plaza, New York, NY 10121-2298. Or contact your local bookstore.

# Dedication

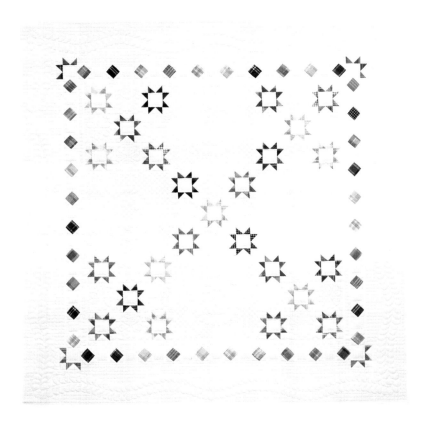

# Contents

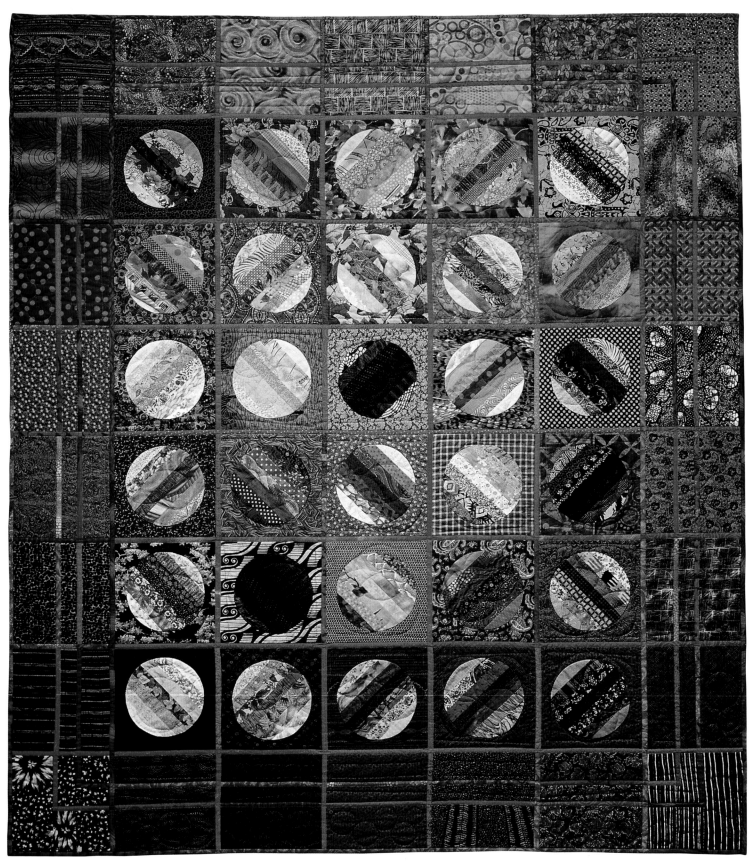

*Ping An*, Melody Crust, 63″ × 73″ (160 cm × 185.4 cm), machine quilted.

# *Preface*

You have just finished your most glorious piecing and appliqué work ever. The quilt top reflects the care and ingenuity you put into creating the pattern and choosing your fabrics. You have sewn each seam using your very best technique. All that is left to do is the quilting, and you hesitate, worried that the quilting design and the stitches may not measure up to the beautiful work you put into your quilt top. You know that to be a quilt, the top must be quilted. But you agonize: What do I quilt where?

You're not alone. Like many quilters, we, too, have experienced that same hesitation and we both have unfinished tops on our shelves to prove it. Yet by taking a creative approach to the quilting and by learning new skills, we have overcome this all-too-common stumbling block. Today, it is rare for either of us to leave a quilt unfinished. In *A Fine Line* we would like to share with you all that we have learned, so your quilt tops are not doomed to stay forever unfinished. Instead, they will take pride of place on the bed or on the wall, where they belong.

Even if you follow a traditional design, no quilt top you make is ever going to be exactly like the pattern, picture, or quilt from which you drew your inspiration. The same is true of the quilting. Just as the choice of colors and fabrics is part of the creative process that makes your quilt top unique, so, too, the choice of quilting design sets your quilt apart. For this reason, our book not only answers the question What do I quilt where? but also explains why certain choices are right for particular quilts. By understanding how your quilting-design decisions affect the look and feel of the finished quilt, you will become comfortable and confident approaching the quilting-design process for each of the quilt tops on your shelves. Even better, you will begin to plan the quilting early—when you are planning the design of the pieced or appliquéd top. In this way, for every new quilt you create, the quilt top and the quilting will be perfectly in tune.

Each of us offers you different skills as you explore creative approaches to quilting design. Heather has designed and primarily hand stitched quilts for more than twenty-five years; Melody, who has taught machine quilting for a long time, understands the particular challenges of quilting by machine. We are both at ease with each method, for we have discovered that some of our quilt tops call for hand quilting while others seem perfect for machine quilting. Perhaps, like us, you will discover that you enjoy both methods. No matter which method you choose, *A Fine Line* will help you create and execute designs that are attuned to the needs of your quilt top.

*A Fine Line* allows you to learn and practice quilting and design techniques in small steps. Because quilting is a visual art, we have provided examples in quilts, stitched fabrics, or sketches for every step. Knowing that new material can seem foreign at first, we have purposefully repeated key information after it has been introduced, often with further examples or illustrations. You will find that this kind of repetition makes learning new ideas much easier. Reading the text and looking at the illustrations are just two ways of learning. We encourage you to try a third way—doing. At the end of each chapter, we have provided short, simple exercises designed to require few materials and little time, so you can practice each new technique quickly and easily.

An innovative feature of *A Fine Line* is a "Let's Play Quilt" section in Chapters Two through Eight. Here, we have chosen a quilt top and share the quilting possibilities that we considered for each quilt. A clear plastic overlay placed on the quilt top can be marked with lines to allow you to see exactly how each design option affects the look of the finished quilt. The "Let's Play Quilt" sections are our way of sharing our thoughts during the design process with you.

In more than twenty years of teaching quilt making we have answered the question How should I quilt this top? for hundreds of students, for hand and machine quilters, and for many styles of quilt tops. We hope that after reading *A Fine Line* you will understand the process of quilting design so you can answer the question for yourself. Then you can stitch more of your splendid tops into well-designed, completed quilts.

Melody Crust

Heather Waldron Tewell

# Acknowledgments

IN THE PREPARATION OF this book, Melody and Heather were fortunate to have the advice of several colleagues who read the manuscript and offered valuable suggestions. They were Cynthia Corbin, Pat Michelsen, and Brenda Shornick. Heather would like to thank Marty Kutz for reading an early draft and offering encouragement. The authors would like to acknowledge the editorial assistance of their husbands, Charles Crust and Duane Tewell, and to thank them for never tiring of the quilting topic.

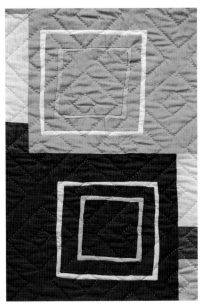

*Sunlight on Flowers*. See full quilt on page 51.

*Mah Jongg*, Melody Crust, 69″ × 62″ (175.3 cm × 157.5 cm), machine quilted.

# CHAPTER ONE

# *Beginning*

For a quilter, few sights are as delightful as the fine lines of stitching that flow into every part of a quilt, holding its layers together. Be they small and subtle, or long and colorful, the stitches are what truly make a quilt. The goal of this chapter is to help you open your eyes to the possibilities in quilting design. Whether you quilt by hand or machine, you will discover that choosing and executing the quilting design is every bit as rich a creative experience as making the quilt top.

Colorful changing-houses line a beach on the Cape Peninsula, South Africa. People tend to see color first, pattern second, and the finer points in a picture or quilt third. In this picture the red, blue, yellow, and green hues are seen first; the repeated shapes of the houses second; and only on closer inspection the texture of the clapboards. Quilters can use this knowledge about people's viewing tendencies to their advantage. When viewing a quilt, delight in its color and pattern, but pause long enough to absorb the beauty of the quilting.

# Creating the Quilting

Greatly simplified, there are two distinct stages in making a quilt. First, you create the quilt top. Second, you quilt it.

Each of these two stages can be further divided into design and execution. You are already familiar with the many design considerations that go into creating a quilt top: choosing colors, fabrics, block patterns, block layouts, borders, and so on. Once you have made these design decisions, you execute them using a variety of skills and techniques.

The same two steps—design and execution—are equally important when it comes to the quilting, the pattern of stitches that hold the three layers of a quilt together. First, you decide upon a design; then you execute it in quilting stitches. *A Fine Line* takes you step-by-step through the design process, helping you explore the many options you have in creating a pattern for your stitches. Along the way, you will also learn practical information that you may find helpful in executing the design, both by hand and by machine, and in finishing the quilt. Our emphasis, however, will be on helping you understand the design phase of the quilting—the process of selecting a successful quilting design for your quilt top.

# Comparing Hand and Machine Quilting

When it comes to visual effect, hand quilting and machine quilting are not necessarily interchangeable. Although machine quilting can be made to resemble hand quilting, each method has its particular look and limitations. These arise from differences in the hand-quilting and machine-quilting processes themselves.

A hand-stitched line is the most subtle of quilted lines. The process of hand stitching dictates this characteristic: stitch by stitch, the hand quilter runs a needle and thread in and out of the layers, leaving a dotted trail. A significant design statement can be made even with a delicate line. People respond to hand-quilted antique quilts, to modern quilts with well-designed patterns stitched by hand, and to innovative quilts that are hand stitched with original designs. The beauty of hand quilting is the quality of the line itself and the texture that the lines create.

The process of machine quilting lays a continuous line of thread on the fabric surface. This line is obvious in a way that a hand-quilted line never will be. Machine stitchers, embracing this quality, have exploited the possibilities of the machine-quilted line. In their quilts, threads in every texture, color, and material are seen as design elements. Innovative lines are becoming part of the visual design vocabulary of machine-made quilts.

In addition to differences in the effect of the stitched line, some designs are simply easier to accomplish with one method than the other. Hand quilters can easily start and stop a line of stitching. Designs with interrupted lines are not a problem for them. Machine quilters, who must secure threads at every start and stop, find these designs tedious. They prefer long lines of continuous stitching. For machine quilters, circles and loops are quickly and easily accomplished using free motion. With this stitching method, disengaging the feed dogs allows the sewing machine's

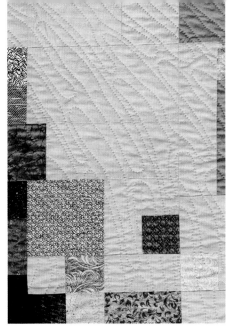

*Beach Rocks.*

Hand quilting creates a series of thread dots and fabric spaces. Quilting stitched by hand creates texture or delicate lines. Designs for hand quilting that incorporate lines that start and stop can be stitched easily. See full quilt on page 71.

*Nababeep.*

Machine quilting leaves a continuous line of thread across the quilt's surface. When stitched with metallic thread, the naturally emphatic line becomes even more noticeable. See full quilt on page 108.

needle to be hand guided as freely as a computer's mouse or a pencil over paper. A hand quilter working with a hoop or frame would have to turn the hoop or body continually or learn to quilt at awkward angles to execute these same designs. The hand quilter will find it easier to stitch quilting designs with gentle curves and less abrupt changes of direction.

Both hand and machine quilting have a characteristic look and certain limitations. Designers of the quilting can learn to use these qualities to their advantage.

## Training the Eye to See Quilting Designs

One of the easiest ways to learn about quilting design is to train yourself to be aware of the quilting whenever you see a quilt. Quilt shops typically have sample quilts on display. Museum collections offer wonderful quilts, both antique and contemporary, for you to study. Viewing antique quilts is an invaluable way to learn about traditional quilting designs. It also helps you train your eye to observe subtle hand-quilted lines.

One of the best places to learn about quilting design is at local and regional quilt shows. We suggest that you tour a show at least twice. In your first walk-through, your eyes will respond naturally to color and pattern. To take in the design of the quilting and the subtle but significant effect it has on the overall look of the quilt, you need to view each quilt a second time.

Notice where the stitching shows and where it is lost. Observe what happens when some parts of a quilt are heavily quilted and others are not. Compare the

*Six Blonde Ladies*; quilt top by Melody Crust, Jill Christenson, Nancy Brister, Kathy Matteoni, Ros Rowley-Penk, Nan Naubert; 50″ × 50″ (127 cm × 127 cm), hand quilted by Melody Crust.

When looking at a quilt for the first time, people tend to respond to color first. The white areas in *Six Blonde Ladies* stand out immediately against the red and green fabrics. Pattern is noticed next. The structure of this quilt is quickly read as having a center block with expanding rings of varying designs. Usually, the last item noticed is the quilting. Simply by becoming aware of your natural viewing habits you can increase your observations of the quilting.

effects of hand quilting versus machine quilting. How puffy is the quilt, and how does it drape? Does the binding or other edge finish add to or detract from the overall look? Does the sleeve fulfill its function inconspicuously?

In addition to seeking out quilts on display, look through quilting books and magazines solely for what the quilts can teach you about quilting design. Use a magnifying glass to see details in the stitching. Observe where straight lines are used, where lines are curved, and where a combination is present. See how the quilting design relates (or does not relate) to the pattern of the quilt top. Be critical. Maybe you do not think every design is wonderful. Try to figure out why a particular design does not satisfy you. You may be surprised at what you observe, simply because you are focusing on the quilting design rather than on the overall effect of the quilt.

You will find that time spent studying quilts from a variety of sources will serve you well when it comes to choosing your next quilting design. Your eye will pick up stitching details you have not considered before. You will begin to understand how the quilting and the design of the quilt top relate to one another. This fresh perspective will help you choose a complementary quilting design for your own projects.

# Sources of Inspiration

The world away from quilts is a rich source of ideas for quilting designs. The wonderful photographs in this book, for example, illustrate how the natural world can inspire a multitude of designs for the quilting pattern. Your own photographs of nature, of architecture, or of cityscapes can do the same. Books and magazines provide an unlimited variety of design ideas. Once you have trained your eye to be aware of subtle lines, you will see quilting designs in carpets, tiles, wallpaper, or even the grain on hardwood floors.

Visit local art galleries and museums. Look, in particular, for ways in which artists use lines and shapes. These details are readily transferable to quilting designs. Sketch elements of any designs that appeal to you, or, if possible, take photographs from which to work.

Magazines of all kinds can be tremendous sources of inspiration. One trick to help you focus on patterns is to hold the magazine upside down. That way, you are not distracted by the overall image and can concentrate on lines and shapes.

Pine bark, Wenatchee National Forest, Washington. A close-up of bark on a ponderosa pine could inspire a quilting design of amorphous shapes.

Seattle, Washington. The architectural shapes of this cityscape easily lend themselves to geometric designs for either hand or machine quilting.

Design inspiration for *Graciela*. Ancient
double doors, Franciscan monastery,
Tzintzuntzan, Michoacán, Mexico.

Keep a binder dedicated to quilting designs. Whenever you make a sketch, take a
photo, or rip a page from a magazine, be sure to save the ideas. You can accumulate
them in a file folder, shoe box, or three-ring binder. With a personally created design
resource, you will be able to capitalize on your past research and will always have a
reference guide of quilting ideas at your fingertips.

# In Review

Whether you quilt by hand or by machine, create traditional quilts as gifts for family
and friends, or stitch nontraditional quilts for personal fulfillment, the design of the
quilting is as important as the pattern of the quilt top to the success of the finished
quilt. In the chapters that follow, we will lead you through the steps that we take
when considering quilting designs for our new quilt tops. You will discover that
opportunities to be creative do not end with piecing and appliqué. Designing the
quilting is also a rich, creative experience.

*Graciela*, Melody Crust, 40″ × 52″ (101.6 cm × 132.1 cm), machine quilted.
The carvings on a Mexican church door inspired the vocabulary of quilting lines on this quilt (see opposite
page). Matching thread color to the background allows the texture of the quilting to predominate over
the quilted line.

# CHAPTER TWO

# Goals of the Quilting

*I*N CHAPTER ONE WE discussed the

importance of the quilting design and how to

train your eye to see it. We also explored sources

of inspiration for design ideas. In this chapter we

discuss the questions to consider before you

begin quilting. Once it is clear in your mind

exactly what you want to achieve in making the

quilt, you are ready to begin.

Pink dawn highlights Mount Victoria over Lake Louise, Alberta, Canada. The red canoes in this picture are clearly the focal point or positive image, while the mountains and water are the background or negative space. Notice that contrast—here of vivid color in a grayed background—draws the eye. For the quilting design, quilters often choose a positive image like a shape and use a background filler pattern such as a checkerboard grid for the negative space. The shape will stand out when the filler pattern contrasts with it. The most effective contrasts in quilting are density of texture and character of line (curves versus angles).

# Preliminaries

Your quilting designs will be fun to stitch and the design satisfying if you ask yourself some questions before you begin:

- Do I intend to hand or machine quilt?
- How much time do I have for this project?
- What is my skill level?
- What use will this quilt serve?

## By Hand or Machine?

As you have already seen, the question of quilting method impacts both how long a design will take to stitch and the form of the design itself. (See "Comparing Hand and Machine Quilting," page 2.) Hand quilting a large project will take considerably more time than machine quilting it. A design for hand quilting can involve many starts and stops and is also easier with gentle curves. Machine quilting works best with long, continuous lines of stitching, but tight circles are easily done. A hand-quilting project is more portable than a machine-stitched one, unless, of course, the sewing machine can come along.

## Time Available?

This question is directly related to the hand-or-machine question. The more time available, the greater the choice in quilting method and complexity of design. The less time until the project must be completed, the more the answer points to a simple design and even to machine quilting.

## Skill Level?

All quilters have times when they are ready to accept the challenge of learning something new and other times when they are happier practicing what they already know. Some quilters have mastered the technique of hand quilting but are just beginning to explore machine stitching. For others the reverse is true: they have successfully quilted some pieces by machine but think that hand quilting is better for a particular quilt top. A third group is equally comfortable with both methods.

Assess your skill level with each quilting method. Think about the energy you have available for learning a new method or improving your skills. Then decide whether you want to quilt by hand or by machine.

This skills assessment will also have an impact on your choice of quilting design. The less familiar you are with the quilting method, the simpler your design needs to be so that you can execute it successfully.

## Quilt's Use?

Deciding how the quilt is to be used will help you be realistic about the amount of time and effort to put into the quilting. First, is it a bed quilt or wall hanging? Is it a functional quilt or an heirloom to be treasured? Will you give it to a child or an

## Options

Set yourself up for success by considering the previous preliminary questions before you begin to design and stitch. A few scenarios will show you how to balance the answers.

**Scenario 1** Dana is an accomplished hand quilter but wants to develop her machine-quilting skills. The quilt is intended as a gift for her six-year-old son. Dana can plan a design for machine quilting that has a combination of long lines stitched with the walking foot or even-feed feature and some curves to be stitched using free motion. Rather than placing the free-motion design in the plain areas, where any mistakes are likely to show, she will be most successful if she practices her free motion in the busy areas and fills the plain areas with beautifully stitched straight lines.

**Scenario 2** Paula intends her quilt for the guest room bed. She has challenged herself to master fine hand quilting with this project, but company will be coming in a few months. Paula has several options. She can stitch long lines on the sewing machine and use hand quilting for areas of fancier stitching. Or she can choose a batting that does not require close quilting and create a design of widely spaced lines, stitching them all by hand. If her design

*Stone Wall Impression #1*, Heather Waldron Tewell, 73" × 51" (185.4 cm × 129.5 cm), machine quilted.

The quilting design on this wall hanging uses one of machine quilting's strengths: tight circles are easy to stitch. With an allover pattern like this, the design can be stitched without marking.

incorporates both straight lines and curves, by the time she has finished the quilt, she will have achieved her goal of improving her hand quilting.

**Scenario 3** Brenda is equally skilled at hand and machine quilting. She is making a wall hanging for her husband's office, but she wants to enter it in a national competition whose deadline is looming. Brenda will more likely make the deadline if she chooses to machine quilt. Knowing this as she works out the quilting design will help her choose patterns that are easy to stitch by machine.

adult? Each of these considerations can have multiple possibilities. For example, a quilt that will be used on a bed but is also intended as a competition entry may have a more complex quilting design than a bed quilt solely intended as a birthday gift for a child.

# A Question of Style

Once the preliminary questions are answered, your next consideration is the style you envision for the finished quilt.

## Techniques

To machine stitch a quilt and achieve the textured look of an antique quilt, follow these steps:

1. Do not prewash your fabrics, but do test for colorfastness. One test is to cut a 2″ (5.1 cm) square of fabric and immerse it in very hot water. Lay the wet square on a white paper towel. If color transfers to the paper towel after 15 minutes, the fabric is not colorfast.
2. Choose a cotton batting that shrinks when washed (read the label).
3. Quilt with invisible thread in the needle and cotton thread in the bobbin. Quilt closely, following the manufacturer's recommended spacing for the quilting lines.
4. Bind the quilt.
5. Wash following the batting manufacturer's recommendation.

If you use fabric and batting that have not been preshrunk, the shrinking will occur when they are washed, resulting in the rippled texture of an old quilt.

## *Matching Authentic Styles*

Some quilt tops fall into well-known categories:

- Amish quilts use solid-colored fabrics in particular color harmonies, as well as quilting in designs such as feathers and cables.
- Welsh quilting is known for its densely stitched quilting designs in spirals and stylized leaf patterns on sateen.
- Baltimore Album quilts are constructed from intricately appliquéd pictorial blocks in rich colors.
- Traditional Hawaiian quilts are made from solid-colored fabrics, using a large-scale, snowflake-like appliqué design.

For quilt tops in a known style, your quilting design choices will come from among the family of designs that supports the particular style of quilt. For example, a Hawaiian quilt is traditionally stitched with echo quilting. If the goal is to create an authentic-looking Hawaiian quilt, then echo quilting should be chosen to maintain the style (see pages 42–43). A little research will lead you to designs that traditionally belong with specific kinds of quilts.

Even if your quilt calls for a particular authentic style, a variety of design choices remains to be made.

## *Nontraditional Style*

If you are seeking a modern look to your quilt, avoid designs that suggest the appearance of traditional quilts, such as evenly spaced parallel lines, grids, feathers, and cables. If you can use these designs with a new twist, you will make a contemporary design statement that will distinguish your quilt from the traditional. Most likely, you will want to develop a new vocabulary of lines and shapes for your innovative quilts.

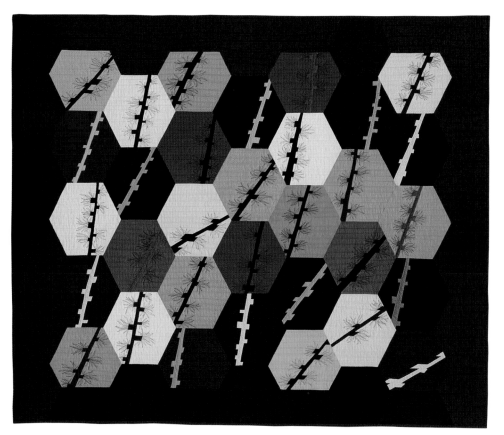

*Larch in Spring*, Heather Waldron Tewell, 77″ × 66″ (195.6 cm × 167.6 cm), machine quilted. The simple quilting design of straight lines across the hexagon blocks highlights the dramatic stitched design of the larch needles. The straight lines are purposefully not evenly spaced or parallel so they do not read like the traditional background quilting design of evenly spaced parallel lines.

## Formal Versus Informal Design

Some quilting design schemes are more formal than others.

Generally, formal patterns stay within the pieced or appliquéd blocks and borders of the quilt top. They have a structured appearance. For example, a quilting pattern that has a floral shape in alternate plain blocks, simple parallel lines across the patterned blocks, and a cable for the border is a formal design. A Baltimore Album quilt with its richly appliquéd wreaths, baskets, lyres, and other pictorial blocks set block-to-block is a style of quilt top that calls for a formal quilting design.

Informal designs tend to be overall patterns that ignore the seam lines and have looseness to them. Both the fan design and the meander are examples of informal patterns. At one extreme, this kind of functional quilting looks like what it is: utilitarian stitching to hold the three layers together. However, functional quilting can be the essence of simplicity. Informal designs are relaxed and often asymmetrical. Scrap quilts are likely candidates for informal quilting design. Another example of an

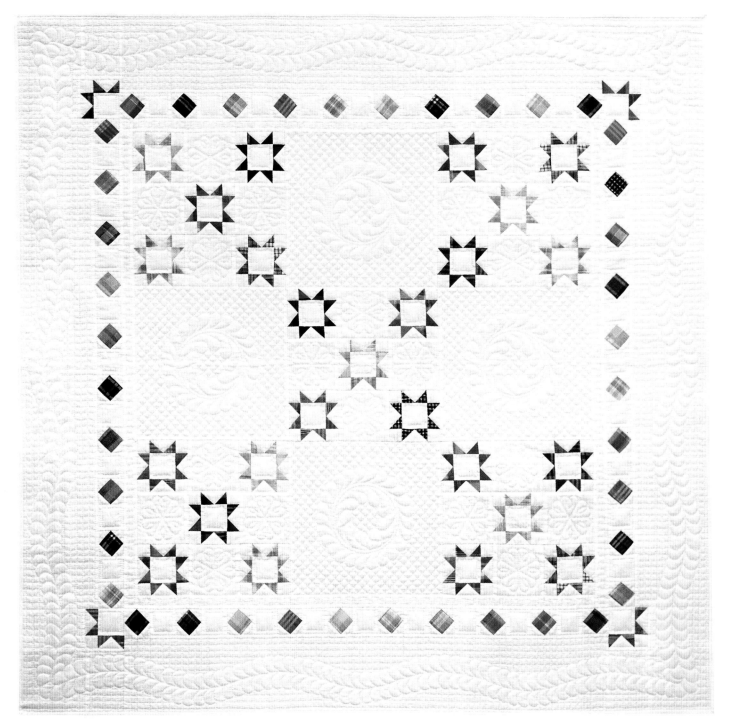

*Plaids in Heaven*, Heather Waldron Tewell, 53″ × 53″ (134.6 cm × 134.6 cm), hand quilted.

This quilt top presents a symmetrical pattern: blocks and pieced block units alternate with white squares. The entire pieced center is surrounded by a wide white border. The formality of the quilt top's design is continued in the formal quilting design. All quilting lines are contained within the seams of each square unit. Small white squares have their own curved pattern to complement the angular pieced stars. Large white squares have an elegant feathered circle. Finally, the outer border repeats the feather motif but this time as a running vine. The vine turns each corner smoothly, sustaining the precision required by formal design.

*Su's Quilt*, Melody Crust, 45″ × 60″ (114.3 cm × 152.4 cm), machine quilted; private collection.

This pieced scrap quilt is appropriately stitched with a relaxed, informal quilting design. Matching threads to the colors of the pieced fabrics blurs the seam lines. A heavy quilting thread was chosen to withstand everyday use.

*Growth Cycle of the Earth*, Heather Waldron Tewell, 24″ × 36″ (61.0 cm × 91.4 cm), hand quilted; private collection.

Solid-colored fabrics and simple piecing convey the growth message of this quilt. The hand stitching in short, slanted lines functions purely to hold the layers together.

informal quilting design, not from the family of linear designs, is shapes scattered irregularly across the surface with a background filler to achieve even density.

For some quilt tops, the choice between formal and informal design will be obvious. Sometimes, either style may be appropriate. In these cases, personal preference and your answers to the preliminary questions on page 10 will be the determining factors.

The process of deciding upon the pattern that will be stitched through the layers begins after the preliminary questions have been addressed. Understanding some general goals that apply to every quilting design will lead to a successful design on your quilt.

*Friends & Relations*, Heather Waldron Tewell, 57" × 71" (144.8 cm × 180.3 cm), hand quilted.

Before quilting, this top was rather formal due to its symmetry. To continue the formal feeling, quilting designs could have been created separately for the pieced blocks, sashing, center appliquéd block, and borders. However, this quilt was intended as a comfy nap quilt for a loved one, so the overall fan design was chosen. This pattern, stitched without reference to the seams, gives the desired informal feeling.

## General Goals of the Quilting

The quilting needs to work with the quilt top's design. It should hold the three layers of the quilt together enough to serve the purpose of the quilt. These objectives can be stated as three broad concepts:

- The amount of quilting should be adequate to hold the three layers of the quilt together. (The quilt sandwich needs to be stitched closely enough to hold the batting fibers in place. How much is adequate depends upon the choice of batting and the function that the quilt will serve.)
- The density of the quilting should be uniform across the quilt surface.
- The quilting design should complement the quilt top.

## The Batting and Its Impact

The first variable in determining how much quilting is adequate to hold the layers together is the quilt batting. Its properties are a significant component in quilt construction and must be taken into consideration when you create the design for the quilting.

Historically, quilts were functional items intended for everyday use. Stitching through top, batting, and backing fixed the batting in place. Unless stitched closely, batting fibers would migrate with handling and washing until loose fibers formed unpleasant lumps inside the quilt. These lumps reduced the warmth of the quilt: wherever fibers withdrew into the lump, there would be only two layers—backing and top.

Our ancestors' solution was to quilt closely enough so that the batting fibers would not migrate. Today, people admire antique quilts for their dense quilting and marvel at the time invested in doing all those tiny stitches. But there was a practical reason behind the stitching: close quilting was needed to prevent fiber migration. Experience told old-time quilters who were stitching through cotton battings that the lines of quilting needed to be spaced no more than ½″ (1.3 cm) apart to hold the batting fibers in place.

Batting has come a long way in modern times. An explosion has occurred in the batting industry both in the materials available and in the manufacturing methods. Materials for batting include cotton, polyester, blends of cotton and polyester, wool, and silk. In response to modern demands for products requiring less stitching, manufacturers have developed methods such as needle punching, bonding, and the use of scrim to fix fibers in place, thus reducing the need for close quilting.

### Terms

"Migration" is the movement of fibers between the layers of a quilt. Adequate quilting controls migration. Batting manufacturers, through innovative processes, combinations of fibers, and the introduction of new fibers such as polyester, have restricted fiber migration of their products, thus reducing the need for close quilting. To learn how closely a batting must be quilted to avoid fiber migration, refer to the label on the batting package.

"Bearding" is the process of batting fibers working their way outside the quilt sandwich and onto the surface of a quilt. These fibers appear as lint and are unsightly. Some battings tend to beard more than others; some battings tend to beard when combined with certain fabrics. The best guides to products that do not beard are discussions with quilt friends and shop owners, as well as your own experience.

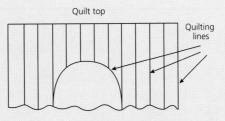

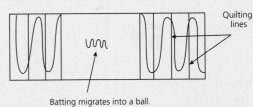

When an area of a quilt is not stitched closely enough and the quilt is handled and washed repeatedly, the fibers in the open area will mat together and form a wad. One hundred percent cotton battings manufactured using older techniques are the most susceptible to fiber migration. The solution is to read the manufacturer's recommended spacing and follow the instructions.

How much quilting will be adequate to prevent fiber migration depends on the batting that you select. The closeness of lines required can vary widely, from ½" (1.3 cm) to 8" (20.3 cm). To learn about recommended spacing of quilting lines for a particular batting, refer to the manufacturer's instructions published on the product's label or go to the company's website. You can also ask at your local quilt shop or talk with experienced quilters. Many books on the process of quilting cover batting properties. See the Bibliography.

When contemplating the design for a particular quilt, you can control how much quilting you will need to do through careful batting selection. You should not select a 100 percent cotton batting that requires ½" (1.3 cm) to 1" (2.5 cm) spacing of the quilting lines if you do not have the time or desire to quilt very closely. This works the other way as well. If you want the soft feel and drape of a 100 percent cotton batting, then as you are designing you need to take into consideration that your quilting design must incorporate a lot of close lines.

## The Importance of the Quilt's Function

The other variable in determining how much quilting will be adequate is the function of the quilt.

Quilts today are being made as wall hangings as well as bed coverings and lap robes. Functional quilts, those used for warmth and comfort, need to be quilted at least as closely as the maximum spacing recommended by the batting manufacturer. By following the manufacturer's instructions, you help ensure that the batting will remain in place through years of handling and washing.

Wall hangings may be quilted more openly than bed quilts. The assumption is that wall hangings will be washed less often, if at all; will be handled less; and do not need to be as strong. As a matter of technical requirement, a wall hanging that will never be washed can be constructed using batting of any fiber content and quilted with widely spaced stitching lines. Even if you contemplate washing the wall hanging only occasionally, quilting following the manufacturer's recommendations for spacing between the quilting lines will be required for the longevity of the quilt.

## Uniform Density

The density of the quilting should be relatively uniform across the quilt surface. Not only does the quilting control fiber migration, but it also controls the puffiness of the fabric on the surface of the quilt. Areas without much quilting ripple and sag, while areas with more stitching lie flat. People all respond to the textural beauty of an antique quilt. Part of the reason is its uniform flatness, which arises from even spacing of the quilting lines across the quilt's surface.

When parts of a quilt are very densely stitched while other parts are quilted minimally, the quilt becomes distorted. Large areas with little quilting sag or ripple unattractively. The greater the difference in spacing of the quilting lines from area to area, the more problems will arise. The edges of the quilt may not be even, and the quilt may not be square.

Pioneer women quilted closely for a practical reason: to prevent fiber migration. With modern battings, today's quilters generally can quilt more openly. They do, however, need to be aware of uniform spacing for the textural beauty that it brings to the quilt's surface.

As you plan your quilting design, strive for a pattern of uniformly spaced lines. We are not advocating mathematical precision. Just be aware that as you open up the distance between your quilted lines, you start to encounter the unquilted fabric's tendency to puff up and ripple.

Like all rules, the rule of uniform spacing can be broken for effect. Now that you know uneven spacing causes distortion and large unquilted areas sag, you can set out to use these characteristics on purpose in a quilt. Your quilt will not have uniform flatness, but that was not your goal for this particular quilt. You may want the shadows that come from sagging fabric. To rise above the rules is a sign of virtuosity.

At the same time that you are thinking about the technical requirements of the materials you will be using, you need to be thinking about the artistry of the design itself.

*Mah Jongg.*
The curly meandering lines stitched with matching machine-embroidery thread emphasize the circular appliqué. The value of the quilting thread was more important than the color. In the darker areas, a dark matching thread color was used. In the lighter center, a light- to medium-colored thread adds texture, providing the viewer something different from far, medium, and close distances. See full quilt on page ix.

## Good Design

The quilting design should complement the quilt top. Simply put, you want a design that looks good stitched through the three layers of your quilt. The quilting design can improve the appearance of a ho-hum quilt top. But the opposite is also true: a poor choice of quilting design can ruin a beautiful piecing job.

Any quilting will change the appearance of the quilt top. To the flatness of the top's surface, stitching through the layers adds texture and, except for in-the-ditch quilting, lines and shapes drawn with the sewing thread. In some cases, the thread will add color as well. The artistic goal of your quilting design is to control the texture and color while introducing lines and shapes that work with the pieced or appliquéd design.

How do you know what looks good? Personal taste and subjective judgment go into any design. Differences of opinion always exist as to what works and what does not. Unless you have entered a competition, in the end you are the only one to say whether your design looks good.

## Techniques

If, in spite of your best design efforts, areas on your quilt puff up unattractively, quilt more lines across these places. Many times, adding a diagonal line or a simple curve through a patch will solve the problem. You can also try repeating a design that is already stitched into the quilt, such as adding a circle within another circle or a square within a square.

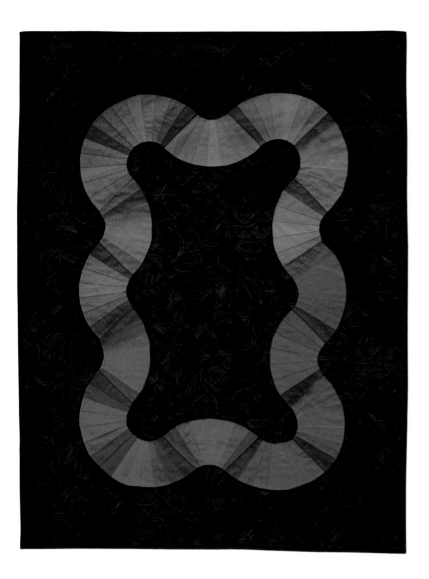

*Rhythm*, Melody Crust, 29″ × 39″ (73.7 cm × 99.1 cm), machine quilted.

The firm needle-punched batting used in this wall hanging required very minimal quilting. The simple diagonal grid holds the layers together without detracting from the pieced design. The fan shapes are not quilted and thus break the rule that the quilting should be evenly distributed over the surface. However, the fan area does not sag because the seams in the piecing add the necessary rigidity.

How can you predict if a design you are contemplating will be effective? One way is to make samples. If you are stitching by machine, samples are easily accomplished. If they increase the likelihood of choosing a design that works, they are worth the time and effort. You can make sampling do double duty by testing batting and thread at the same time. If you are hand quilting, samples are possible but excessively demanding in time.

A good way to try out designs for the quilting is to draw them first on a sheet of clear plastic. Art supply stores sell .004 mm plastic, which is inexpensive and comes in two sizes: 2′ × 3′ (61 cm × 91.4 cm) and 4′ × 6′ (121.9 cm × 182.9 cm). Clear plastic shower-curtain liners are another possibility, but we have found that

*Tropicana*, Melody Crust, 40″ × 55″ (101.6 cm × 139.7 cm), machine quilted; private collection.

This quilt (see opposite page), intended as a gift for a family with young boys, needed to be cozy and sturdy. It also needed to be finished quickly. The quilt was made with a needle-punched cotton batting and heavy machine-quilting thread. Using a free-motion quilting design that could be stitched without marking and long straight lines done with a walking foot, the materials and techniques met all of the goals.

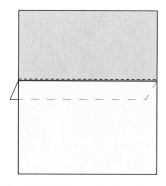

"In-the-ditch" refers to stitching that runs along the low side of a seam, where there are no seam allowances, and close to the seam line. Machine quilters will find that straying accidentally across the seam line is very easy. Hand quilters have a different problem. For hand quilters, the presence of the thick seam allowances makes stitch formation more difficult. From a design standpoint, stitching in-the-ditch adds little to the quilt. In fact, it can accentuate rippling at seam lines. When stitching in-the-ditch is the only quilting, no texture will be added, and texture is the beauty of a quilt. Other, equally simple patterns will make a more effective completed quilt.

Stitched sample for *Country Brambles*. One goal of this stitched sample was to practice creating the thorns along the canes and the serrated edges of the leaves without first drawing them. Another objective was to determine which red and green threads would be most effective. The third goal was to determine if uneven parallel lines in thread matching the background fabric would work in combination with the stitched cane and leaf design. See full quilt on page 33.

the smaller-sized plastic makes it more likely that we will take the tool off the shelf and use it. You will also need a wet erase marker in a color that shows against the fabrics in your quilt top and a damp rag for removing the lines. (A dry erase marker also works but has objectionable fumes.) Prepare your overlay by covering the outer edges with masking tape. The tape makes a visible frame to avoid accidentally marking on your quilt top.

Spread your quilt top right side up on a table. Place your prepared plastic over it, covering the different areas of your quilt top's design. For large quilts, fold the top in quarters so that the plastic covers the center area as well as the borders. By considering all parts of the quilt top at once, you will more likely create an integrated quilting design.

Draw the quilting pattern that first comes to mind. Don't worry about perfectly smooth curves or straight lines. Strive for the effect of the design you have in mind. If you don't like the design, simply wipe it away with your damp rag, and try something else. If you have a stencil or pattern you are considering, trace it on your plastic, position the plastic over the quilt top, and evaluate the design against your quilt. Sometimes, a purchased stencil or pattern in a book is the perfect size. More often, the design needs to be enlarged or reduced to fit the space on your quilt better. You can audition different background filler designs in the same way.

Although you may think your first design is good, try to come up with several more. By stretching yourself, you may discover an even better solution.

*Plum Pudding*, Heather Waldron Tewell, 50″ × 62″ (127 cm × 157.5 cm), hand quilted.

The beauty of this hand-quilted design comes from the closeness of the stitched lines and from the precise fitting of the feathered design into the pieced border. The fancy quilting is placed where it will show: on the solid-colored fabric. To maintain the close density of the quilting, simple straight lines are stitched through the patterned fabrics of the stars.

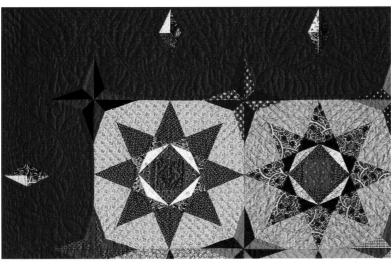

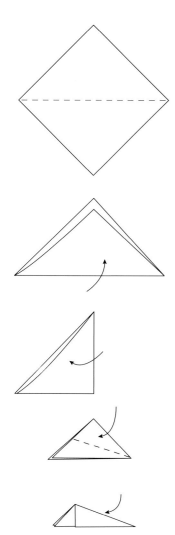

To fold a snowflake for cutting, complete these steps:

1. Start with a square of paper.
2. Fold it in half diagonally.
3. Bring the points at the ends of the long side together, forming a right angle.
4. Do this again.
5. Bring the 90-degree corner down to the longest side.

# In Review

The three general goals of the quilting are interdependent. Quilting that is technically enough to hold the layers together is not necessarily pleasing to the eye; it may not be artistically satisfying. Except with batting that requires very dense quilting, more quilting than the manufacturer recommends will likely result in a more beautiful product and longer-term pleasure.

Knowledge is the secret to a well-designed quilt: knowledge of the interaction of the quilt-top design with the quilting, of the amount of stitching required by the batting you choose, and of the effects (whether you see these as good or bad) of inadequate stitching. With knowledge, you can predict the stitched results of your quilting design, and you will be pleased with the finished look of your quilt.

Now that the preliminary questions and background objectives are well in mind, you can examine some specific categories of quilting patterns for their design potential. The exercises that follow will help you see the quilting and apply the general objectives of the quilting designs.

1.  Begin a notebook of quilting designs. Go back through old magazine issues and either photocopy or tear out examples of designs you like. Go through the quilt books in your library, focusing on the quilting. Photocopy or sketch the designs that appeal to you; make a notation of where you found the design in case you want to refer to the original picture in the future. When you go to a quilt show, pay particular attention to the quilting designs. Take photographs (if allowed) that capture the quilting design. You may want to make some sketches as well, since it is very difficult, even under favorable circumstances, to take photos that adequately show the quilting. Place this material in a three-ring binder or photo album, and keep adding to it.

2.  Cut three sheets of thin paper such as newsprint or computer paper into 8″ (20 cm) squares. Fold each in half four times diagonally, with the last fold being the 90-degree corner down to the longest side. Using paper scissors, cut only straight lines out of the folded sides of the cone-shaped paper. The shapes cut away will be triangles or rectangles. Unfold the paper. Pretending that this pattern represents your quilting design, observe the placement and sizes of the holes and the widths of the paper intersections in relation to the holes. Are they uniformly spaced? Are the sizes relatively even? Cut another snowflake using only curved lines; the cut-away shapes will be half circles, ellipses, or squiggly shapes. Unfold the snowflake. Study the pattern for its density. Also note the different effect that all straight lines versus all curves gives to the design. Cut the last snowflake using a combination of straight and curved cuts. Unfold and study. (Note: Most snowflakes do not make good designs for stitching. As cutouts where the paper and the holes are visible, the designs are exciting; when stitched into a quilt, however, they lose definition.)

3.  Collect a pile of magazines, preferably on nonquilt subjects like gardening or home decoration. Turn one magazine upside down, and open to any page. Examine how the page is broken up spatially. Are there big shapes and little shapes or all one size? Where is the focus and what makes it? How do areas of text relate to photographs? Turn the pages of the magazine, and try different types of magazines, seeing how the pages are divided. Tear out any pages that have potential, and place them in your design notebook.

For an informal look, the quilt can be stitched with an overall design. While a straight-line design is easy to do, it will add more straight lines to the straight lines in the piecing. A better choice is a pattern that adds a contrasting kind of line, such as the fan. (In the sketch, machine stitching lines are blue; hand quilting lines are black.) An even density will be taken care of easily because the fan is a naturally uniform design.

Before selecting designs for the stitching, consider these key questions: What quilting method do I want to use? What is my skill level? What time do I have available? and What is the quilt's style?

The quilt makers decided to stitch by machine. Because they are accomplished stitchers, degree of difficulty is not an issue. While time is not particularly important, the quilt will not be an heirloom either. A moderate amount of quilting is appropriate. The quilt top is not a recognizable style, nor is it clearly formal or informal, so there are no constraints in the quilting design relating to matching a style.

A more formal approach is to create patterns that stay within the two blocks: the red and brown squares, and the blue and white stars. For hand quilters, simple bisecting of the squares in the red blocks will fill the space nicely. A circle can be stitched in the red center squares.

For the star areas, the circle idea can be repeated in the corners. Outlining inside the star points enhances this interesting shape, but more quilting is necessary in the center for uniform density. A square with an X or a circle with an X are two possibilities. Hand quilters will have to take special care when stitching through the middle of the star.

Finally, designs for the outer off-white triangles, both the ones along the four sides and the ones in the corners, need consideration. By repeating squares and circles already planned, these areas will be integrated into the entire quilt top design.

*(continues)*

The machine quilter's version of the previous hand-quilting design would be to transform the individual circles into a continuous looping design. The isolated circle in the middle of the red blocks has been eliminated and a boxy design is substituted. This quilting plan is easily produced by machine using a combination of walking foot (or even-feed feature) and free motion. The entire design can be done without marking.

Another idea is to superimpose a curved quilting design over the red blocks. The design suggested is easy to stitch by hand. A machine quilter with good free-motion control will be successful with this design, too. The straight lines for the star blocks contrast well with the proposed curved design for the red blocks.

These two motifs will need to be supplemented to raise the density. The squares at the corners of the star blocks need more quilting. One solution is to add a line parallel to the line that bisects the square. The off-white triangles along the outer edge need more quilting, too. Repeating the diamonds here will tie the pattern into the blue stars, but a few more lines of stitching will be needed to flatten the quilt uniformly.

Building on the same idea, the looping motif has moved to the red blocks and is given a little variety by increasing the size of the loop as it crosses the centers of the blocks. The rest of the red block can be stitched with two overlapping rectangles. Using a lightweight thread in a value close to the value of the the patch ensures that a thready appearance will be minimized.

For the star, outlining that previously led to a diamond shape has become a rounded loop. The imprecise loops across the red blocks allow the loops across the blue stars to be less precise as well. The background

of the star blocks can be stitched with some straight lines, repeating the squares of the quilt top.

For the outer triangles, repetition of motifs led to simple parallel lines and a long looping motif to frame the entire quilt.

For this quilting design to be adequate to prevent fiber migration, the batting needs to have a manufacturer's recommended spacing of no more than 2" (5.1 cm) because some areas in the red blocks will not be dense enough for battings requiring very close lines of quilting.

***American Pie***, **Melody Crust and Heather Waldron Tewell, 39" × 52" (99.1 cm × 132.1 cm), machine quilted.**

The finished quilt, stitched using the looping design in the bottom left sketch on page 26, demonstrates the complementary pattern of curves and angles. Texture, not stitched line, shows on the red blocks and star blocks because the threads match the patches over which they are sewn. The stitching pattern is more obvious in the outer triangles because these areas are constructed of light-colored fabrics. For the looping line around the quilt, pins placed at even distances maintained the proper spacing of the loops for free-motion stitching without the necessity of marking on the quilt top.

# CHAPTER THREE

# Exploring a Simple Line

*A* LINE IS THE building block of all

quilting designs.

What the quilter can and cannot do with a

line stitched through the layers is both the

challenge and the limitation of quilt making.

While a painter can make a mark from the

thinnest hairline to the broadest sweep by the

choice of tools—a fine brush or a floor broom—a

quilter stitching through the layers can use only

needle and thread.

Amber-colored light in Antelope Canyon, Page, Arizona. A line is the most basic unit of design, but that is not a limiting factor. Lines can be thick or thin, delicate or bold, straight or curved, twisted or languid, and an infinite variety of other expressive forms. People respond with positive emotions to the undulating lines in this sandstone.

The stitched line can be augmented in various ways, such as by using buttons to create the line, couching yarn, or stitching with a double needle. However, the basic design element of the quilting is still a line. When a line starts and stops at the same point, the most that can be made is the outline of a shape. Shapes will be discussed in the next chapter.

Five qualities exist simultaneously in every stitched line. These qualities are

1. visibility
2. character
3. length
4. direction
5. scale

Understanding the many qualities of a line enables you to expand the potential designs for a particular quilt. You can come up with many ideas by intentionally varying each of these qualities. The more you play around with the possibilities, the greater the likelihood that you will find a linear design that suits the particular quilt perfectly.

## Visibility

The visibility of a line sewn by hand and a line stitched by machine varies widely. Knowing in advance how much a line will or will not be seen at a distance and how much texture the stitching will add to the surface takes the guesswork out of the design process. Creating a design with this knowledge leads to greater satisfaction with the finished quilt.

### Hand Quilting

Rocking the needle in and out of the quilt sandwich, the hand quilter creates a series of thread dots and fabric spaces on the surface of the quilt. The look of this line is a subtle, bumpy indentation. Even with contrast between the value of the thread and the value of the patch over which the stitches run, the thread itself rarely dominates. At only a few paces from the quilt surface, the observer will read texture, not line and color, unless the contrast is nearly as great as white thread over black fabric.

A subtle line is the unique element of hand stitching.

"Value" refers to the relative darkness or lightness of a color. For example, pink and scarlet are both in the red color family. Pink, being pale, is a light value of red. Scarlet is a darker value of red than pink. Compared with black, scarlet is a medium value. The value of a color is only as light or as dark as it appears in relation to a neighboring color.

*Russian Snowflakes*, Heather Waldron Tewell, 53″ × 65″ (134.6 cm × 165.1 cm), hand quilted.

Hand quilting creates two textures on this quilt. In the tan border the pattern is the circular teacup design borrowed from traditional quilt making, with the addition of some grid lines to increase the density of the quilting. Hanging diamonds, also an old pattern, is stitched behind the irregular snowflakes. The remaining areas of the quilt have simple angled lines to maintain the even density. The pleasure in this hand-quilted design comes not from the eye following a line of stitching but rather from the texture of the stitched patterns.

## Techniques

For the hand quilter, the quilting line can be made more visible—that is, less subtle—in several ways:

- Increase the contrast between the thread and the patch it crosses. The contrast can be between the color of the thread and the color of the patch, as when red thread is sewn on a blue patch. The contrast can be in value. An example is navy blue thread introduced over an ice blue square. Both kinds of contrast can be used together—yellow (a color naturally light in value) thread sewn over eggplant-colored fabric. In practical terms, even thread that greatly contrasts with the fabric will only slightly increase the visibility of the hand-stitched line. Because the stitches of fine hand quilting will always be a series of thread dots and fabric spaces, the line created will never be as obvious as a line of machine stitching.

- Increase the length of the stitches. Laying more thread on the surface of the quilt, especially if the contrast between the thread and the fabric is great in color or value, will make the hand-stitched line stand out. "Big stitch"—stitches that are about ¼" (0.6 cm) long with short spaces between—has become popular on folk-art quilts, either as the only quilting stitch or as an accent with other stitching. These stitches can stand out.

- Use a thread heavier or shinier than hand-quilting thread, such as perle cotton or a metallic thread. These threads have their drawbacks. Perle cotton can be difficult to pull through the fabric layers, and metallic thread tends to fray and break

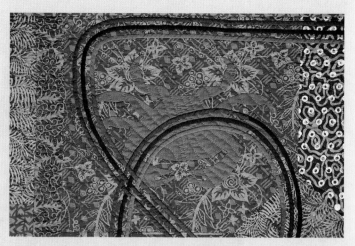

*Dungeness in the Eelgrass.*

Off-white quilting thread crosses over patches of medium value. Because the line is hand stitched, even though there is contrast between the value of the thread and the value of the patches, the quilting is seen only as texture until it is viewed closely as in this detail. See full quilt on page 99.

at the eye of the needle (it is not a strong thread). Although embroidery floss is readily available, comes in a wonderful array of colors, and appears to be strong because the bundle of threads is so thick, be wary of using it as a quilting thread. Embroidery floss is soft and does not wear well.

- Stitch another line of quilting ⅛" (0.3 cm) or ¼" (0.6 cm) away from the first line. Note: The line that the eye will follow is not a line of quilting but the fabric channel created between parallel lines of stitching.

## *Machine Quilting*

Machine stitching places a solid line of thread on the quilt top interrupted only by the merest dimpling where the bobbin thread loops up to form the stitch. Because of this very different process, much more thread is apparent with machine quilting than with hand quilting. Even when invisible thread is used, the line itself is crisper than the soft dots and dashes of hand quilting. Unless the machine quilter chooses to soften the effect by controlling the color, value, and weight of the thread, the look of machine stitching is the line itself. By using thick thread, a contrasting color, or both, the machine stitcher can virtually draw with the sewing machine.

An emphatic line is the essence of machine quilting.

Hand stitching and machine stitching produce very different but equally rewarding types of line.

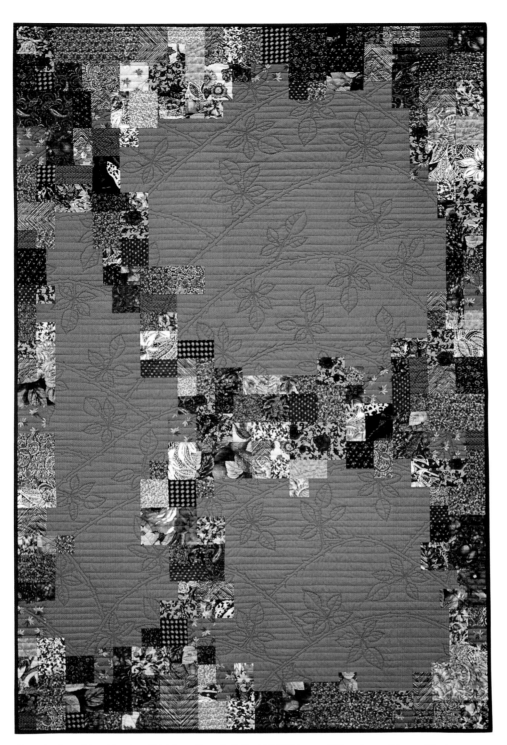

*Country Brambles*, Heather Waldron Tewell, 50″ × 74″ (127 cm × 188 cm), machine quilted.

Canes and leaves of blackberry brambles are drawn with the sewing machine using free-motion technique. The pattern stands out because the machine lays a continuous line of thread on the quilt's surface. Thread color is also a factor. Burgundy-tinted brown thread—darker than the rust background— was used for the cane and leaf outlines. A light-colored thread in pea green was used for the leaf veins. The same design stitched by hand would not be nearly as visible.

Machine quilting can be done with one of two methods:

1.  Attach a walking foot or engage the even-feed feature of the sewing machine. With this help, the sewing machine will evenly feed the thickness of the three layers. You set the stitch length on your sewing machine's gauge and determine the direction of the stitching by moving the fabric with your hands. This method is best for the straight lines and gentle curves of machine quilting.

2.  Drop the feed dogs (the little toothed bars just visible underneath the throat plate of your machine that feed the fabric under the needle) and attach the darning foot. With the feed dogs disengaged, the sewing machine is in free-motion mode. The advantage of free motion is that the quilt need not be turned at all when creating the stitched design. Circles, curlicues, leaves, and all manner of curved designs can be created with ease. The disadvantage is that you yourself must maintain an even stitch length. Beautiful free-motion stitching takes practice, but the fun of doing it is well worth the effort in learning how.

A machine-stitched line by its nature is very visible. The line can be made progressively less obvious in these ways:

- Choose a lighter-weight thread. From heaviest to lightest, threads run from machine-quilting thread (40 weight) to regular sewing thread (50 weight) to machine-embroidery thread (60 weight). The bigger the number is, the lighter weight the thread.
- Use a thread that matches the patch. When the thread and the patch are the same color, the thread blends into the patch.
- Use a thread that is both lightweight and a matching color to blend the stitching line even more.
- Sew with invisible thread. Invisible thread takes on the color of the fabric, leaving only a quilted texture.

## Disappearing Lines

So far, we have presented a line as being consistently visible or subtle. A "sometimes" option is also possible. When thread crosses over fabrics of different colors or values, the line may blend with some patches and not with others. For example, if red thread travels across a white patch and then across a red patch, the line is easily seen against the white fabric but gets lost against the red.

The disappearing effect can be controlled by careful choice of thread. Stitching with the same thread across patches of many different colors or values makes the line come and go. Changing thread color to match each patch crossed maintains a consistent visibility for the quilted line.

When changing thread colors is not practical, two options are possible:

1.  For machine quilters, use invisible thread—smoke for quilts with predominantly dark fabrics, clear for others.
2.  For machine or hand quilters, choose a value of gray or beige thread that blends with all the different fabrics in the quilt top. Stitching a sample will tell you whether gray or beige will work to achieve the visibility of line desired on a particular quilt.

As a designer, you have to decide how much come-and-go you can tolerate. In some cases, you will want to alter the quilting design to maintain the same degree of visibility for the stitched lines.

Another way of creating the "sometimes" option is to use multicolored thread. This thread is available in values ranging from light to dark (variegated) or from color to color (color-blocked) on the same spool. When the thread is stitched into a quilt, the effect is that some parts of the line disappear and other parts stand out. This come-and-go visibility engages the observer's attention when chosen for effect.

For design purposes, sometimes a visible line is desired, sometimes a more subtle one. Good design involves choosing the technique that suits the visibility goal, altering the technique or materials to most closely achieve the goal, or changing the design so that the visibility goal can be reached.

## Techniques

A line of machine stitching can be made more obvious in these ways:

- Increase the value contrast between the thread and the fabric.
- Increase the color contrast between the thread and the fabric.
- Increase the thickness of the thread. A heavier-weight thread can be run through the needle of the sewing machine or couched onto the surface. Special threads can be wound onto the bobbin with the quilting done upside down (that is, from the back) so that the design thread (laid down by the bobbin thread) ends up on the front of the quilt.
- Combine all or some of the preceding suggestions.

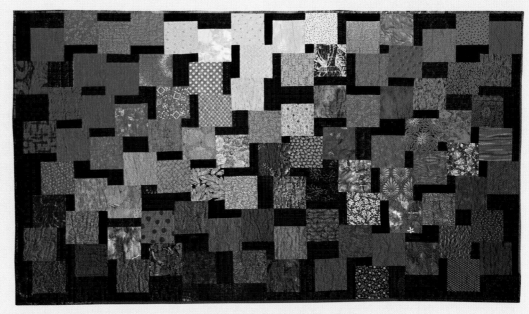

*Sundown*, Melody Crust, 70″ × 40″ (177.8 cm × 101.6 cm), machine quilted.
The machine-embroidery thread used in this piece was carefully chosen. Thread matches patch in both color and value to sustain the same texture over the entire quilt.

- Use a double needle for stitching, laying down two lines at the same time—in effect making a thicker line. Be aware when choosing this design that double-needle stitching lays a zigzag line on the back of the quilt.

*Old Growth and Salal*, Heather Waldron Tewell, 89″ × 61″ (226.1 cm × 154.9 cm), machine quilted.
Disappearing lines can be used for effect. The overall design of salal leaves carries out the Northwest forest theme. Stitched entirely with green thread of medium value, the quilting is visible over dark or light patches but is lost against medium-value fabrics. With this come-and-go effect, the machine quilting does not dominate but still has a presence.

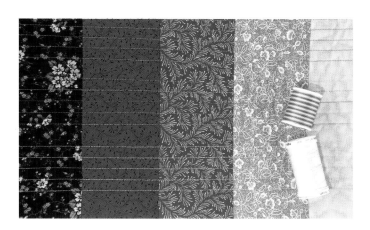

Stitching a small sample is a good way to test whether or not a gray or beige thread will blend adequately with all the fabrics on the quilt top.

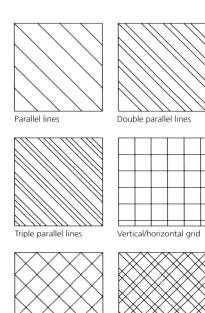

Parallel lines

Double parallel lines

Triple parallel lines

Vertical/horizontal grid

Diagonal grid

Plaid

Hanging diamonds

Basket weave

The family of traditional straight-line designs includes parallel lines, double parallel lines, triple parallel lines, vertical/horizontal grid, diagonal grid, plaid, hanging diamonds, and basket weave.

# Character

Lines come in many styles or characters.

## *Straight*

A straight line is the most basic style. Inventive pioneer quilters came up with a wide variety of easily stitched straight-line patterns for their bed quilts. Parallel lines and grids with variations of each have been the most often repeated. Because of their timeless beauty and ease of stitching, quilters use them today.

To be in keeping with old-time quilt tradition, place evenly spaced straight lines parallel or at a 45-degree angle to the seam line.

For an innovative look, try varying the spacing, the orientation, or both:

- While keeping lines parallel, use uneven spacing.
- Stitch straight lines at an angle greater than or less than 45 degrees to the seam line.
- Combine the two preceding suggestions.
- Stitch straight lines that are not parallel to each other.

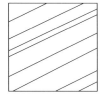

Innovative ways to use straight lines, resulting in a nontraditional look to the design, include uneven parallel lines, lines placed at a different angle than 45 degrees to the vertical or horizontal axis, and a combination of these—lines both uneven and not at 45 degrees.

Lines that are not parallel will move closer and closer together at one end and farther and farther apart at the other. Radiating lines are a particular kind of nonparallel lines. At the center, the lines are densely spaced. The farther out from the center, the wider apart the lines become. Because the general goal of the quilting is for even density across the surface, nonparallel lines need careful placement. Either use them over short distances where the variation in spacing is not too great, or make the slope between the lines shallow so that they do not converge or get too far apart across the quilt.

## Curved

Lines can be curved. The family of curved lines includes some from traditional quilt making, like clamshells and fans, as well as the inventions in contemporary quilt making, like curls, folds, squiggles, spirals, leaf vines, and an infinite variety of other wonderful bent lines. Each of these lines can be manipulated until its character suits a particular quilt. The curves themselves can be tight or loose. They can turn frequently, infrequently, or not at all.

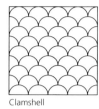
Clamshell

Fan

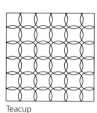
Teacup

The clamshell, fan, and teacup are curved-line designs commonly found on traditional quilts.

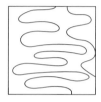

Innovative curved lines will look very different depending upon whether the curves are tight or loose, or repeat frequently or infrequently.

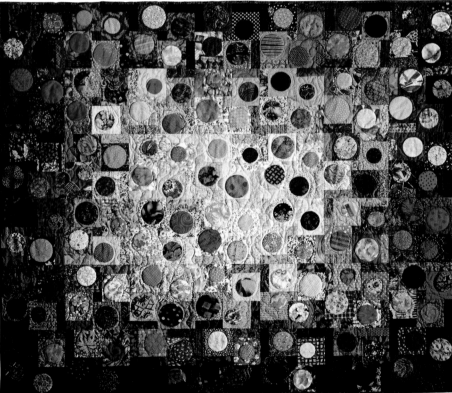

*Prayer Beads*, Melody Crust, 59″ × 50″ (149.9 cm × 127 cm), machine quilted; private collection.
These free-flowing curved lines complement the curves and angles in the piecing.

*China Rose*, Melody Crust, 45″ × 54″ (114.3 cm × 137.2 cm), machine quilted; private collection.
The evenly spaced lines and boxy, angular appearance of the Greek key design complement the blue labyrinth piecing. Changing the size of the key designs gives variety while maintaining unity.

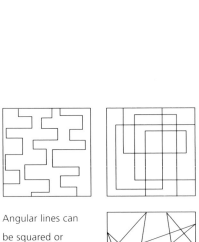

Angular lines can be squared or pointed; they can repeat regularly or irregularly. Notice the different feelings that these three patterns of angular lines evoke.

## Angular

Lines can be angular. Jagged, jerky, zigzag, boxy, triangular, or spiky all describe angular lines. As with curves, the angles can be varied: wide or narrow, evenly repeated or repeated irregularly.

## A Combination of Angles and Curves

The same line can be a combination of both curves and angles. Or, an angled line and a curved line can be combined on the same quilt. Combination lines can be very interesting to the eye, but they can also appear busy. Use the design overlay described in Chapter Two to audition your linear design before stitching.

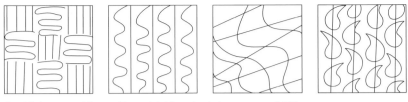

Combining curved lines with straight lines leads to more possibilities.

*Frolic*, Melody Crust, 24″ × 36″ (61 cm × 91.4 cm), machine quilted; private collection.

Although the top consists of square and rectangular shapes, a mix of curves and angles is used in the quilting to increase variety. Curved lines from top to bottom are continuous to hide starts and stops in the binding. Simple straight lines were used in the light squares to minimize busyness. Matching thread color to the fabric adds to the receding-background illusion.

Curved meander,
not crossed

Angular meander

Curved meander,
crossed

Rock meander

Meander curves
combined with angles

Meanders come in all kinds.

# Length

Another quality of a line is its length. Long lines and short lines have different design effects. As a matter of technique, construction is different by hand than by machine.

## *Continuous Lines*

Some quilting designs consist entirely of one long line. Starting at point A, the line travels over the entire quilt surface until it stops at point B. The purest example is meander quilting (also called stippling). The machine lends itself easily to this design. The frequent changes of direction in the usual meander make execution by hand tedious, although some old-time quilters and even contemporary ones use it for effect in small areas around stuffed work.

Basic meander stitching consists of curves that are both evenly spaced and the same size. In traditional meanders, the line never crosses. But this rule should not be followed blindly. Crossed lines can be interesting, too. The variety of meander designs, both crossed and not crossed, is endless. By creating an innovative meander pattern, you add originality to your work, setting it apart from quilts that repeat the same stipple pattern over and over.

*Wildfire.*

Serpentine stitching by machine in the background blends the blocks. Stitch length and width were adjusted to please the eye. A simple, long zigzag is stitched through the circles to suggest flames. This angular line contrasts with the running curves of the serpentine. See full quilt on page 136.

## *Repeated Lines*

Overall designs in traditional hand quilting and most background filler designs are the same line repeated many times. Unlike continuous-line designs, repeated lines use more than one line to form the pattern. The many designs invented by pioneer hand quilters are prime examples of repeated-line designs: diagonal parallel lines, double parallel lines, fans, clamshells, diagonal grids, on-grain grids, hanging diamonds, teacups, chevrons, echo quilting, and so on. Some of these designs are straight-line designs and some are curved.

The repeated character of these lines, requiring numerous starts and stops, is not the obstacle in hand quilting that it is in machine quilting. The machine quilter will want to be sure to have start-and-stop technique well mastered and the quilting designed so that starts and stops are reduced in number as much as possible.

Other examples of repeated-line designs are the stitching patterns programmed into modern machines—zigzag, satin stitch, serpentine, to name a few. The serpentine is the stitch most often used successfully as a quilting line. Because programmed stitches like the serpentine are done with a walking foot, they are good choices for the quilter who is not confident of free-motion stitching.

## Techniques

When machine stitching starts or stops away from the outside edge of the quilt so that the start or stop cannot be secured beneath the binding, one of two methods can be used to fasten the thread ends, depending upon the design involved:

1. If the design is a shape, that is, starts and stops at the same point, begin the line of stitching with about ¼" (0.6 cm) of tiny stitches. Change to your favorite stitch length, and stitch the shape. After returning to the starting point, continue stitching directly over the small anchoring stitches, using the longer stitch length for about ½" (1.3 cm). Then secure with tiny stitches for about ¼" (0.6 cm) directly on top of the longer stitches. Long stitches will disguise the anchoring stitches at both the beginning and ending of the line.

Method 1.

2. When starts and stops do not overlap, bring both ends of the thread to the back, knot the threads, and bury the knot in the batting. To save an extra step when knotting the ends, make the first stitch (one down/up with the sewing machine needle) about 1" (2.5 cm) from the line to be sewn. Pull the tail of the bobbin thread to the top (an old sewing machine needle

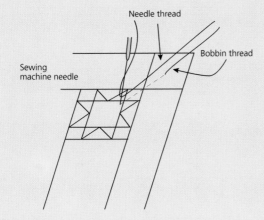

Method 2.

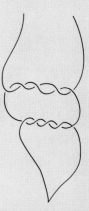

Needle thread

Loop of bobbin thread

works well as a tool). Holding both top and bobbin threads securely with your fingers, reposition the sewing machine needle at the true starting point and stitch the design.

At the end of the line of stitching, lift the presser foot, pull the quilt to one side, and cut the top thread 3" (7.6 cm) to 4" (10.2 cm) long. Cut the bobbin thread, leaving a 3" (7.6 cm) to 4" (10.2 cm) tail.

To tie a knot at the beginning of a line of stitching, turn the quilt over. The 1" (2.5 cm) section of bobbin thread will lie on the quilt back. Pull the 1" (2.5 cm) stitch to expose a loop of top thread and bring it to the back. Tie these ends into a "surgeon's knot," formed by making a square knot with two turns in the loops. Be sure to make successive loops in opposite directions. Thread the ends in a large-eyed needle or self-threading needle and bury the knot. Trim excess thread.

Tying a knot.

To secure the threads at the end of a line of stitching, bring the top thread to the back by pulling on the bobbin thread. Knot with the surgeon's knot; then bury the knot and tails as before. A self-threading (also called easy-threading) needle saves time in the knotting process, which admittedly can be lengthy on a heavily stitched quilt.

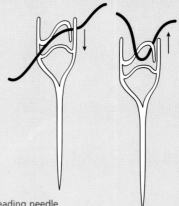

Self- or easy-threading needle.

Whether stitching by hand or machine, be careful if you are thinking of an overall checkerboard for your quilting pattern. This design can easily make your quilt look like a mattress pad. Try doubling or tripling one or more of the lines to make a plaid motif instead.

Another example of a repeated-line design is echo quilting. For this design, many lines make concentric rings growing ever larger around a motif. The quilted line repeats the contour of the appliquéd or pieced patch. Echo quilting is the traditional background quilting for large-scale Hawaiian quilts.

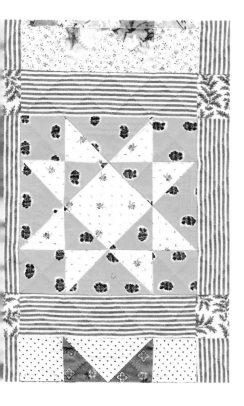

*The Gem*, Heather Waldron Tewell, 40″ × 52″ (101.6 cm × 132.1 cm), hand quilted.

The main quilting pattern consists of a diagonal grid. The pattern has been interrupted and filled in with either multiple parallel lines or double X lines, so the design does not read as a mattress pad.

Part of the elegance of echo quilting is in the uniform spacing between successive lines. With practice, hand quilters can gauge the distance by eye, using a pin now and again as a guide. To achieve uniform spacing with free-motion stitching on the sewing machine without marking, use the edge of the darning foot as a guide.

## Direction

Lines of hand and machine quilting have direction: up and down, left to right, corner to corner, or around in circles. Choosing vertical lines as opposed to diagonal or horizontal lines can make a difference in a design's effectiveness. Horizontal or flat lines give a sense of stability and calm. Diagonal lines imply motion and can add tension. Vertical lines suggest energy.

The same kind of line that changes direction can add interest to the quilting pattern. On traditional quilts, repeated lines of parallel stitching often change direction along the outside border.

## Scale

In addition to visibility, character, length, and direction, lines of quilting have scale. Scale refers to the distance between the lines. Lines can be placed very closely together or they can be spaced widely. Close spacing can look tidy

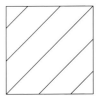

The distance between lines, or scale, has a significant effect on the look of the design. Consider several possibilities and choose the one that best suits the particular quilt.

as well as tight; wide spacing can appear airy or hurried. The effect depends upon how that spacing looks on the specific quilt top. The same spacing will not be right for every quilt. Indeed, the same spacing may not be right for all areas of the same quilt.

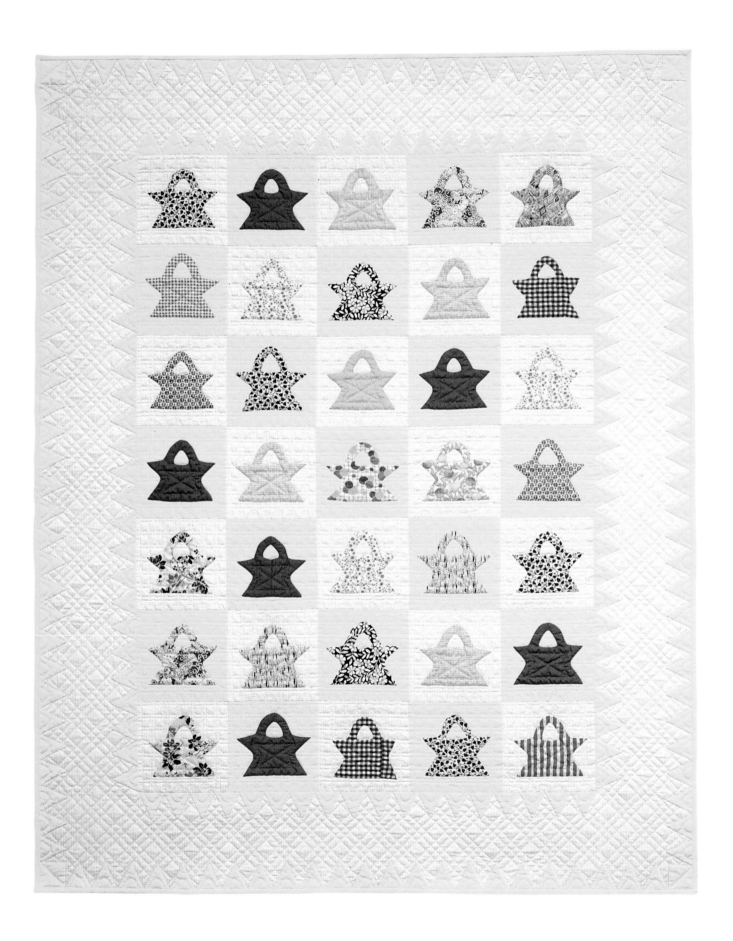

Try out several spacings for your lines, using the design overlay recommended in Chapter Two, to determine the one or a combination that works best. If you play around with different spacings, your eye will tell you when you have come up with the most pleasing set of lines for your quilting design.

## In Review

A linear design may be the overall stitching pattern for the entire quilt surface, or it may be just one of many designs that combine to make up the stitched pattern. When thinking about a linear design for a particular quilt, play around with it for a while. Vary each of the five characteristics of a line—visibility, character, direction, length, and scale—until you find the look of the line that suits the quilt exactly. The exercises that follow will help you explore the quilting possibilities that each of these characteristics offers.

1.  Draw three checkerboard grids on three large sheets of tracing paper. Space the lines ½″ (1.3 cm) apart, 1″ (2.5 cm) apart, and 1½″ (3.8 cm) apart. Lay the different scales of grids over an appliquéd block. See which scale seems right for that block. Also, turn the drawn designs so that they read as diagonal designs, then as vertical/horizontal ones. Evaluate the effects of these different orientations. Try out the different grids and orientations on another quilt block. Do you like the same spacing and orientation for both blocks?
2.  Find ten pictures of quilts representing different qualities of lines. Search for variety in all five aspects: visibility, character, direction, length, and scale. Copy the pictures (if possible), label them with the qualities of line that they represent, and place them in your design notebook.
3.  Using pencil and paper (computer paper works well and is inexpensive), create a series of meander designs: curved, angular, a combination, and a continuous leaf. Lines may cross or may not. They may be truly one continuous line filling up the sheet of paper, or they may be several lines. Maintain the contact of pencil with paper to simulate machine free-motion stitching. Remember to keep the designs evenly dense. Your first efforts probably will not please you. Often, just by sticking with the exercise you will come up with a pattern that, with a little revision, will be a workable design.

*Connecticut Baskets*, Heather Waldron Tewell, 48″ × 62″ (121.9 cm × 157.5 cm), hand quilted. The major motifs hand quilted on this traditional quilt (see opposite page) are two slightly different straight-line grids. The grid around the baskets consists of two lines close together plus a space, making a minimal plaid. For the grid in the border, the lines are spaced farther apart, and three are repeated instead of two. This plaid feels more open than the grid around the baskets, because the lines are spaced more widely. The grids are not oriented the same: the two-line grid is vertical and horizontal, and the three-line grid is on the diagonal. Variations in the grids add interest to the quilted texture, while their general similarity maintains the unity of design.

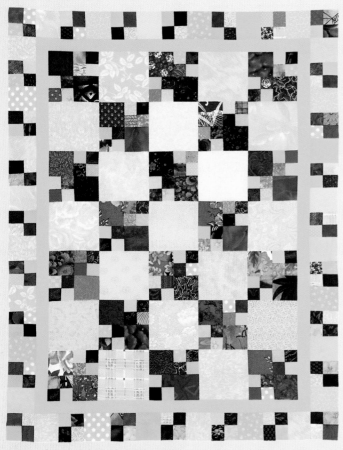

An overall linear design composed strictly of straight lines can easily be executed by hand or machine. The sketch shows a design based on diagonal lines that includes some variation in the spacing of the lines. Lines form a close checkerboard in the plain squares, where the intricacy of the quilting will have the most impact. At the same time, these are straight lines repeating straight lines in the piecing. How about introducing some curves to contrast with the pieced design?

*Lemonade* is a traditional quilt block (a Double Four-Patch) rendered in nontraditional vibrant colors. This duo style will allow the quilting to go in either a traditional or nontraditional direction. With 1" (2.5 cm) squares positioned consistently in the same direction in the center field, the set gives a decided diagonal movement to the quilt top.

The basic units of the quilt top's construction are

1. the pieced four-patch block
2. the alternate plain block
3. the narrow yellow border
4. the outer border of pieced four-patch units alternated with plain blocks

Because this is a small piece, perhaps the preliminary questions about hand or machine quilting, time available, and skill level are not as important.

A cable pattern is a motif from traditional quilt making. It is also a design with a linear feeling, like the pieced pattern in this quilt. The cable can be stitched by hand or machine, following the diagonal motion of the quilt's set. If it is stitched by hand over the pieced blocks, crossing over the many seams will require care. If the design is stitched by machine, this problem will not exist. Choosing a value of thread that matches most of the patches will make the machine-stitched line disappear, leaving only quilting texture behind. On the other hand, choosing a thread that contrasts with the fabrics will make a more definitive statement of the quilting motifs. The choice is up to the quilt maker.

A combination of straight and curved lines is shown between the diagonal cables. These lines are necessary to fill out the density of the quilting design. The curves can, of course, be more precise than the sketch indicates, if that design aesthetic is desired.

This quilting design repeats the previous pattern of cables alternating with straight and wavy lines but places the interesting elements of the design—the complex cable—across the alternate plain blocks. For the hand quilter, the new placement is significantly easier to stitch because it avoids many more seams. The cable will stand out better across the plain blocks, both because the yellow fabrics are rather light and because these areas are not busy with piecing or printed with high-contrast motifs.

Stitching angular and curved free-form linear designs will move the quilt away from a traditional feeling toward a contemporary look. Reinforcing the diagonal set, the boxy designs can be stitched over the plain blocks and a spiral, curved design over the pieced four-patch blocks. Notice that the spirals and boxes are not carbon copies. This adds an element of design "aha" to the surface as well as frees the stitcher from having to be precise.

Careful attention to the spacing of lines in the boxes and curves in the spirals will assure that the quilting is evenly dense. A personal response to the question Do you like the feeling of the spiral with the multiple boxes? will determine whether this quilting pattern complements the quilt top's design.

*Lemonade*, Melody Crust and Heather Waldron Tewell, 26" × 34" (66 cm × 86.4 cm), machine quilted.

The machine quilting, stitched following the sketch on the top left of this page, was done exclusively with yellow machine-embroidery thread and a walking foot. Strips of tear-away paper, enough for all design repetitions, were cut for the cable designs. The cable was marked on the top layer with a permanent-ink pen; then all the paper layers were stitched through with a large unthreaded needle and small stitches. To minimize starts and stops, the cable was stitched with continuous parallel lines, creating a checkerboard effect rather than the woven design typical when hand quilting a cable.

# CHAPTER FOUR

# Adding Shape to the Mix

*A* SHAPE IS CREATED when a line begins and ends at the same place. Shapes can be used in many ways in the quilting design. One shape can be repeated as the design element. Two or more shapes can be combined to form the quilting design. Shapes can also be paired with a linear pattern that fills the area around them. A shape can be as simple as a circle or as complex as the architectural detail on a classical building.

Red hydrangea leaf, Washington Park Arboretum, Seattle, Washington. Observers are drawn to this picture by the glorious color. Also note the bold feeling that the leaf takes on because of its scale—its overwhelming size in relation to the whole picture. Notice the details of the veins and the jagged outside edge. A leaf such as this can inspire a unique quilting design.

A shape is a line that starts and stops at the same point. A simple shape can be made more demanding by increasing the changes of direction that the line makes. A complex shape has many changes of direction but only one starting and ending point.

Start/stop

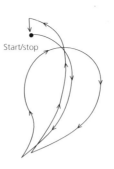

Start/stop

Start/stop

*The Green Flash.*

The uncomplicated circular shapes accent the simple piecing. These shapes were not adequate to provide the even density to secure the quilt together, so the black areas were quilted with straight filler lines. The concentric circles also serve to repeat the sun theme. See full quilt on page 68.

*Geometry in the Fields*, Heather Waldron Tewell, 61″ × 42″ (154.9 cm × 106.7 cm), machine quilted.

The design for the machine quilting is simply the outline of a leaf shape with a few internal veins. The leaf shapes are placed side by side, with some change of direction.

# Simple Shapes

Some shapes are uncomplicated forms such as circles, squares, diamonds, or rectangles. These simple shapes can be used by themselves for the quilting design.

One possibility is to place the shapes side by side. With a regularly spaced pattern on the quilt top, the shapes may align perfectly. With different-sized patches, irregular spacing, or both, the hand quilter may need to make some adjustments to avoid stitching through seam allowances, which can be a problem because of the extra thickness.

If the simple shape does not make a dense enough design when repeated by itself, a denser design can be created in several ways:

- Reduce the size of the repeated shapes.
- Overlap the shapes.
- Repeat the same shape in concentric rings.
- Add some filler lines inside or around the shape.

*Sunlight on Flowers*, Heather Waldron Tewell, 57″ × 70″ (144.8 cm × 177.8 cm), hand quilted; private collection.

Because the squares and rectangles in the piecing and appliqué vary in size, cookie-cutter squares in the quilting design placed parallel to the vertical and horizontal edges of this quilt would inevitably have involved some stitching along seam allowances. To avoid this problem, the design was placed at a slight angle. Lines of hand stitching cross over seam allowances nearly on the bias—much easier to stitch. The effect is of the repetition of quilted squares over pieced and appliquéd squares but with the added ease of stitching.

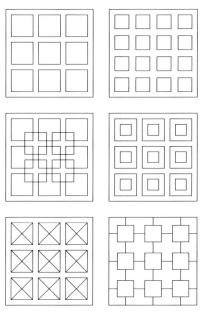

The same shape can be repeated in a great variety of ways to increase the density of the stitched lines.

*Ping An.*

The circular shape is repeated in a variety of ways. The main blocks are quilted with overlapping circles in different sizes. The border sections are quilted with the same overlapping circles resized to fit the border spaces. See full quilt on page vi.

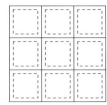

Outline stitching for hand quilters is done ¼″ (0.6 cm) inside seams. This placement assures that stitches go through only the quilt top, batting, and backing and not through the seam allowances. Tiny, even stitches are difficult through more layers. Although machine stitchers have no difficulty sewing through greater thicknesses, for a traditional look they will want to maintain the ¼″ (0.6 cm) spacing when outlining.

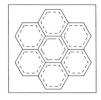 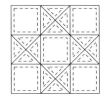

Grandmother's Flower Garden is a one-patch design. Outlining results in an evenly dense design of regular hexagons. Outline quilting a Variable Star block results in two shapes: squares and triangles.

# Multiple Shapes

Simple shapes can be used in combination to add variety. Squares can be alternated with circles, or circles can be stitched inside triangles.

In essence, old-fashioned outline quilting where stitching travels ¼″ (0.6 cm) inside the seam line of all the patches results in a quilting design of simple shapes. Depending upon the patches, the shapes may be all the same, as in Grandmother's Flower Garden, or they may be different, as when an Ohio Star pattern composed of triangles and squares is outline quilted.

*Lady of the Lake*, Heather Waldron Tewell, 72″ × 88″ (182.9 cm × 223.5 cm), hand quilted. Hand quilting in the small triangles outlines the patch. Simple outlining of the large triangles would not have been dense enough. Not only would the fabric have sagged, but these areas also would have been uninteresting in comparison with the liveliness of the many small triangles. Instead, applying the principle of contrast, a circle fills the large square, with additional stitching in the corners and across the inside of the circle to maintain a uniform density of stitching.

Outline quilting in its simplicity may be a good design when the quilt top is already busy with complex piecing, many colors, great value contrast, and a variety of prints. In this case, an elaborate quilting design would not show and may detract from rather than add to the overall look of the finished quilt.

When considering outline quilting, take a look at the size of the patches. Some additional quilting may be necessary through the largest ones to maintain an even amount of stitching across the entire quilt surface.

## Complex Shapes

Complex shapes are a combination of many shapes together, as a bunch of grapes consists of many spheres. The classic example from traditional quilt making is the family of feather designs. Other designs include animals, birds, lizards, and alphabet letters.

Most complex shapes do not work well repeated side by side or concentrically. Generally, they are paired with a filler pattern. The filler serves as a vehicle to highlight the complex shape.

## Shapes and Filler Patterns

Many designs from traditional quilting combine a shape with a background filler pattern. The shape is usually curved, similar to a feathered wreath, and the background design is usually geometric, most often a checkerboard or grid design. On appliquéd quilts the appliquéd motifs may take the place of the curved quilting design. The combination of shape and background filler has become standard in quilt making because it works. The pairing results in quilting that is visually easy to read when stitched and has interest as well as variety.

What makes this pairing successful? In the context of shape and background filler, quilting creates a sculpted relief. Unlike crafters of other sculpture media such as wood, stone, or clay, the quilter cannot remove the background material to reveal a raised motif. Instead, the background must be flattened to make the motif stand out. This is done with stitching. Analysis of old quilts using shapes and background fillers as their quilting designs reveals the following:

- These designs are evenly dense.
- Lines of the background fillers are slightly closer than the lines creating the shapes, making the shapes stand out.
- Curves of the shapes contrast with straight lines of the background fillers, making the design easily understood at a glance.

Often, for ease of stitching, machine quilters pair a curved meander as background filler with a curved-shape motif. The tightness of the meander compensates for the lack of contrast in character between the filler and the shape.

Whether you're using designs of one shape, combinations of several shapes, or complex shapes with background fillers, each shape's proportion, placement, and method of execution are important considerations in the ultimate design.

*Plaids in Heaven*.
The feathered wreath is just as beautiful today as it was when the first pioneer stitcher used it on her quilt. Paired with a background design of a small-scale grid, the curved design stands out well. The quilting is highlighted because the fabric is a solid of light value. See full quilt on page 14.

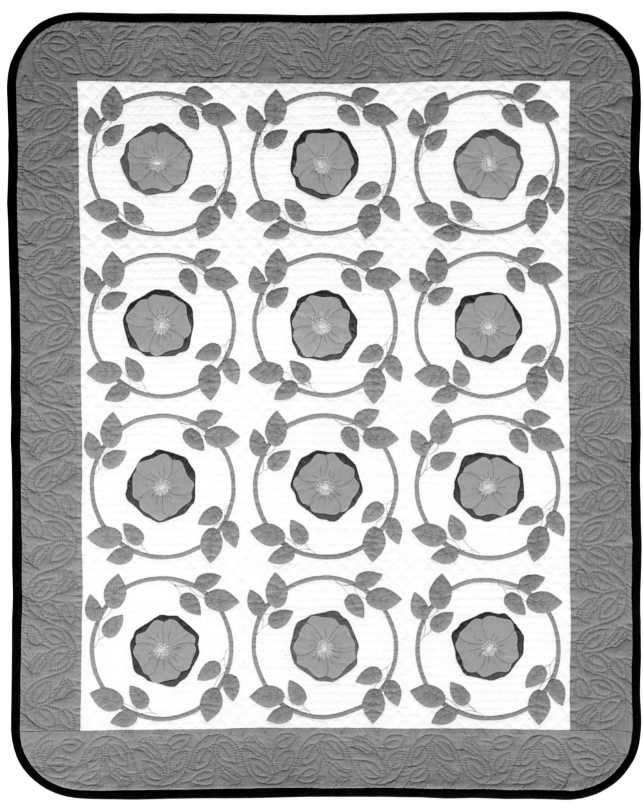

*Rose Wreath*, Heather Waldron Tewell, 39″ × 49″ (99.1 cm × 124.5 cm), hand quilted.

The shapes in the appliqué take the place of a curved quilting pattern and contrast with the geometric
grid in the quilting surrounding the wreaths.

The curves of a loose meander tend to blend with the curves in the shape motif. The design will stand out better when the meander is tight in comparison with the curves in the shape motif.

## Proportion

When designing a shape, be sure to consider the size of the shape in relation to the space it is to fill. To avoid stitching through the seam allowance, hand quilters will want to design their shapes so that they stay ¼″ (0.6 cm) inside the seam line. A shape that is too small may seem like a bull's-eye or appear insignificant. A shape that is too large may overwhelm the motifs surrounding it. The perfect size is not a mathematical equation but rather what pleases your eye in relation to the other design elements of the quilt. With the modern copy machine, designs can easily be enlarged or reduced, allowing you to try out different sizes until you find the one that pleases you.

Right-handed quilters will find it easier to stipple by machine if they go clockwise. Left-handed quilters will want to go counterclockwise.

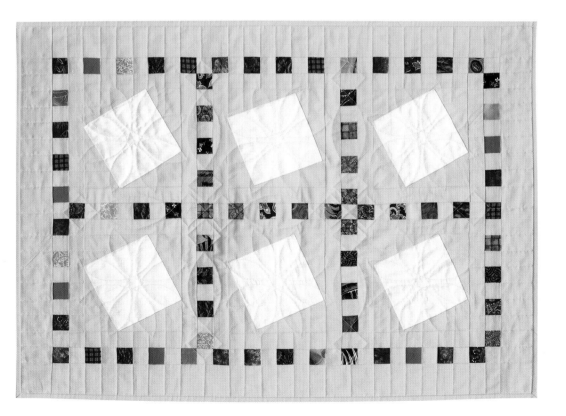

*Gold Fields*, Melody Crust, 32″ × 23″ (81.3 cm × 58.4 cm), machine quilted. The oversize floral shape accents the straight piecing while adding needed complexity to the quilt. To ensure even density, parallel straight lines start at the shape and extend to the quilt's edge. The yellow machine-embroidery thread blends with the background fabric.

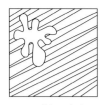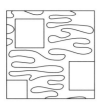

Nontraditional placement of shapes in a space includes off-center and scattered placements. A background filler around or between the shapes will, in most cases, be needed to keep stitching lines relatively uniform across the surface.

# Placement

Historically, shapes were centered in a space. To maintain a traditional style, use the center orientation for the shapes. For a contemporary effect, try placing shapes asymmetrically or sprinkling them over the surface. Some background filler will likely be necessary to achieve an even density of quilting.

# Shapes by Hand or Machine

Shapes are ideally suited to hand quilting. The hand quilter begins, stitches along, and stops back at the beginning point to create a shape.

The issue for the hand sewer is the size of the shapes. Small shapes present difficulties. Think about stitching a series of circles created by drawing around your spool of thread. The design may create an interesting texture, but stitching each circle will involve multiple rotations of the entire quilt. The smaller a shape, the more frequently the quilter will have to turn the hoop or body while sitting at a frame, to maintain a comfortable angle of stitching. These adjustments take time, which could have been spent stitching, and they can be annoying and frustrating.

*Blue and Brown Churn Dash.*
The narrow border is quilted with a circular design marked by tracing around a coin. These circles are very small. The design, stitched one circle at a time, was tedious to do. See full quilt on page 70.

When choosing the size of a shape, the hand quilter must strike a balance between the practical aspects related to the shape's size and the design effect desired. The stitcher may decide that a small shape is important to the design and therefore worth the extra time it takes to execute. On the other hand, the small-scale design might be abandoned in favor of a shape or linear pattern that is faster to accomplish.

Whereas size is the main issue for the hand quilter when thinking about shapes as a quilting design, starts and stops are the main issue for the machine quilter. Every time a line of machine stitching starts and every time the line ends, top and bottom threads must be secured. These starts and stops take time, which is why machine quilters favor longer, continuous lines.

Books on the process of machine quilting give detailed explanations on how to secure the threads (see the Bibliography) or review the techniques on page 41. No matter how you secure the ends, the goal is to make the starting and stopping as inconspicuous as possible. Unsightly starts and stops will detract from an otherwise well-designed and well-executed quilting pattern.

The machine stitcher has three choices when creating a quilting design of shapes:

1. Be confident of your starting-and-stopping technique and go for it.
2. Plan a design with larger, more complex shapes to reduce the number of starts and stops.
3. Revise the repeated-shape design into a continuous-line design.

Machine quilters have been inventive in converting shapes into continuous-line designs. Concentric circles and squares have become rounded and squared spirals.

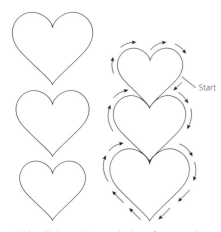

Changing from a design of repeated shapes to a larger, more complex shape on the same theme is another possibility.

With a little revision, a design of repeated shapes can be changed for stitching in a continuous line by machine.

Repositioning the shapes so that they touch, and rethinking the order of stitching, may lead to the solution.

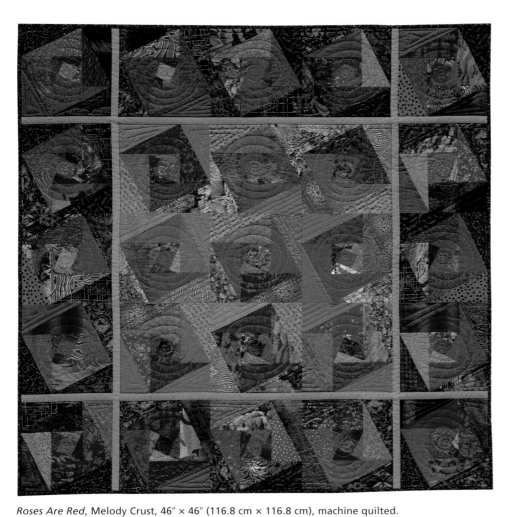

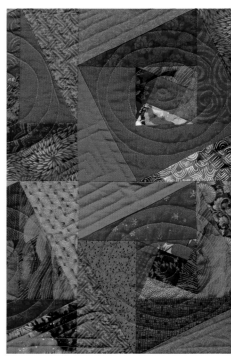

*Roses Are Red*, Melody Crust, 46″ × 46″ (116.8 cm × 116.8 cm), machine quilted.

Both square and circular spirals were used here. The round shapes accent the square piecing and give the flowers some life. The square forms provide even density and blur the background piecing.

Quilting feathers by hand involves just a little traveling inside the layers to get to a new starting point.

One possibility for machine stitching is to retrace the lines of the feathers.

Another option, which avoids the double-stitched line but creates a less traditional feather design, is to open up the spaces between the individual feathers.

Feather designs have been handled in two ways: either by retracing lines or by opening up the pattern. By playing around with pencil on paper, you may be able to convert your next design to a longer, continuous line for easy machine stitching or faster hand quilting. After all, starts and stops take time for a hand stitcher, too.

## In Review

Shapes from simple to complex, with or without background filler patterns, provide a wide variety of quilting designs. The exercises that follow will help you use shapes.

1. Draw a series of shapes side by side: cookie-cutter animals, maple leaves, chili peppers, or a design of your choosing. Draw all the images right side up or alternate with upside-down images. You might also repeat the designs in a circle. Placing tracing paper over your master pattern and using a pencil, see if you can come up with an interesting pattern that retains the character of the shapes but becomes a continuous line for hand or machine stitching. Remember to consider the density as you design.

2. Cut three squares out of scrap paper (newsprint works well), one 18″ (45.7 cm), one 12″ (30.5 cm), and one 6″ (15.2 cm). Draw a 6″ (15.2 cm) circle on tracing paper, and hold it over each square. Does the square seem right in all three places? Too big? Too small? Draw a 6″ (15.2 cm) complex shape from a stencil or quilting pattern book onto tracing paper. Hold this shape over the center of each square. Does your idea of what is too big or too small change? Enlarge or reduce the complex shape until it seems the right size for each square. Are the sizes different?

3. Draw nine 3″ (7.6 cm) squares on a piece of paper. Make a small circle (a dime works well) in the center of each square. You can change this circle to a flower or star shape if you like. Create many different background filler designs around each central motif, noticing how the filler affects the design. Ideas for background fillers are vertical parallel lines, horizontal parallel lines, a vertical/horizontal grid, a diagonal grid, hanging diamonds, clamshells, teacups, and meanders.

# Let's Play Quilt: *Wild Rose*

A simple quilting solution is to stitch an overall linear design across all four areas of the quilt. Diagonal lines or a grid are two possibilities. However, with so much plain background, the quilt top seems to call for a more interesting quilting design. The fan pattern is visually more complex while remaining easy to execute. Fans can be stitched by hand (shown as repeated black lines) or by machine (shown as continuous blue ones). Stitching an overall design without regard to piecing or patches was frequently done on traditional quilts. The overall fan design is an acceptable design solution and gives a traditional yet informal look to the quilting. If this quilt were larger with more plain areas, however, this stitching pattern might not be interesting enough.

The Whig Rose block appliquéd in characteristic red and green on muslin and its center placement put *Wild Rose* in the family of traditional-style quilts. Choosing quilting patterns from traditional quilt making will enhance the quilt's traditional feeling.

The quilting plan needs designs for four main areas:

1. the appliquéd patches
2. the background behind the appliquéd block
3. the inner border, which is the same size all the way around the quilt
4. the outer border, which is wider on the top and bottom than on the left and right

Another solution is to repeat elements of the appliqué as shapes for the quilting. For hand quilting, small roses can be stitched in the inner border with stems and leaves rearranged to fill the horizontal space. These motifs frame the center medallion block. The wide border at the top and bottom is the place for a design from the family of traditional motifs. A feathered wave or a cable will work equally well. The motif can cross the top and bottom outer border only, or it can be created as a narrower design so that it can go all the way around the quilt. A similar design of shapes can be created for stitching by machine.

*(continues)*

With shapes filling only part of the area to be quilted, a background filler is necessary to increase the density of the quilting. Choosing a filler that contrasts in character with the curves of the shapes will help make the shapes stand out. Any of the straight-line designs will work: parallel lines, double parallel lines, or a simple grid. Because this quilting design consists of considerable filler in relation to a few shapes (including the appliqué), changing the direction of the background lines as they travel across the quilt surface increases the visual interest of the overall design. Using double parallel lines will further increase the complexity.

Machine stitchers can translate repeated lines suggested for the hand-quilting design into continuous lines, quilting curves or straight lines over the large leaves, small leaves, and roses. Although several alternatives are suggested in the sketch, the same quilting design should be repeated on the same shape of patch to maintain the symmetry of the quilt's overall design.

Outlining the appliquéd motifs by hand will add to the stitching density, but some quilting across the largest patches in the center medallion will also be necessary. These patches will ripple unless stitched through. More stitching may also be required if the batting needs close stitching lines, as when a 100 percent cotton batting is used. The sketch suggests several different designs that repeat curved or straight lines already present in the appliqué. Any one of these will be equally effective.

For ease of stitching, machine quilters may make different design decisions than hand quilters. For example, a larger shape such as the pointed flower motif from the center of the appliquéd block can be the repeated shape instead of the small rose. To maintain the traditional style and add pattern to the quilting, feathers can be stitched in the outer borders using free motion. The suggested background filler is simple straight lines but with changes of direction from vertical and horizontal to diagonal. The vertical and horizontal lines frame the center medallion and keep the stitched flower motif from floating in space. While starts and stops will be necessary with this design, having the straight lines continue over the center medallion reduces their number.

As the sketch demonstrates, a few more lines around the central red flower will be needed to maintain the even density of the quilting.

*Wild Rose*, Melody Crust and Heather Waldron Tewell, 33" × 41" (83.8 cm × 104.1 cm), hand quilted.

Hand quilting using traditional design motifs of parallel lines and a multistrand cable, as in the top left sketch on page 60, completes this simple piece. Close spacing of the background lines makes the quilted flower shapes and cable stand out. The appliquéd patches were first outline stitched and then filled in with simple lines.

# CHAPTER FIVE

# Planning the Design

**T**HE BASIC GOAL IN creating a quilting design, as discussed in Chapter Two, is to find a stitching pattern that will hold the three layers of the quilt together in a satisfying way. Stitches can add depth and texture, highlighting elements in the quilt top design. Simply stated, the quilting design should complement the quilt top.

Red and purple tulips dominate the landscape, Skagit Valley, Washington. This picture is immediately enjoyable because of its design. The photographer has framed the view to use the principle of repetition. Parallel lines are repeated in the foreground and background, but they change direction from horizontal to vertical. One kind of plant is pictured, but they vary in size. The dominant flower color is red, but there are both orange reds and purple reds. Often, repeating the same line or shape with variety will lead to a successful, unified quilting design.

Keep the following points in mind when designing the quilting:

- The amount of quilting should be adequate to hold the three layers of the quilt together. The closeness of the quilting depends upon the batting selected and how the quilt will be used.
- The density of the quilting should be relatively uniform across the quilt surface. By keeping this objective in mind, you will ensure that no unquilted areas will sag (unless, of course, this effect is part of the design aesthetic for the particular quilt).

## Highlighting the Quilting

Stitching through the layers is a time-consuming process. Although machine quilting takes less time than hand quilting, a significant amount of time is involved in both processes. For this reason, a general rule to keep in mind is If it won't show, keep it simple.

*Dandelion*, Heather Waldron Tewell, 43″ × 68″ (109.2 cm × 172.7 cm), machine quilted.

On the front of this whole-cloth quilt, the stitching design shows well because the fabric is a solid and a light value. As the back demonstrates, the same design is nearly lost when stitched over patterned fabrics.

Quilting does not show well on fabrics with

- a lot of pattern (busy fabrics)
- many different colors
- medium-dark to dark value
- a combination of these characteristics

Nor does an intricate quilting motif show well when stitched over a block with a busy pieced or appliquéd pattern.

Because the visibility of a line of quilting is partially due to the shadow the indentation makes on the fabric, white and very light fabrics highlight the quilting most effectively. Quilting shows best on fabrics with

- no pattern or very little pattern
- little color variation
- light value
- a combination of these characteristics

For example, a solid fabric will show off quilting better than a print of the same value. If the solid is also light in value, the quilting will show even better.

Time-conscious quilters will plan intricate designs for places where they will show. Simple designs that are faster to execute can be stitched over areas where the quilting will be less visible.

## Possibilities for Design Placement

Unless a quilt is constructed from one whole piece of cloth, every quilt has multiple components that can be looked at singly or in various combinations as areas for distinctive quilting-design elements.

A design can be created for

- an individual patch
- several adjacent patches
- one block
- several adjacent blocks
- the entire quilt surface
- one border or several borders

As part of the decision making for the quilting, consider ignoring the seams and crossing over patches, over seams between blocks, and even over the entire quilt surface. Try out several ideas using the design overlay described in Chapter Two before choosing the one that pleases you most. Open yourself up to the possibility of new quilting schemes.

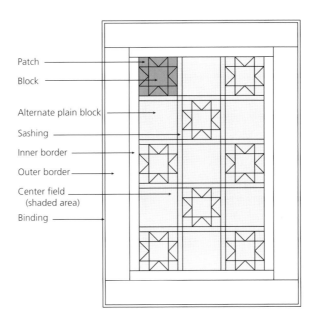

Patch
Block
Alternate plain block
Sashing
Inner border
Outer border
Center field (shaded area)
Binding

This diagram identifies the major parts of a quilt. During the planning of a quilting design, the parts can be thought of as separate units, or they can be grouped together in various ways. Whichever way the design is approached, all the quilting designs must work together.

## One Patch or Several Patches

Generally, quilting designs that fall within one patch reinforce the construction lines of the quilt top. This type of purely functional quilting is most effective when the quilt top itself is interesting due to the pieced pattern and fabric choices. Other times, however, making the seams more obvious through the quilting can lead to a dull presentation.

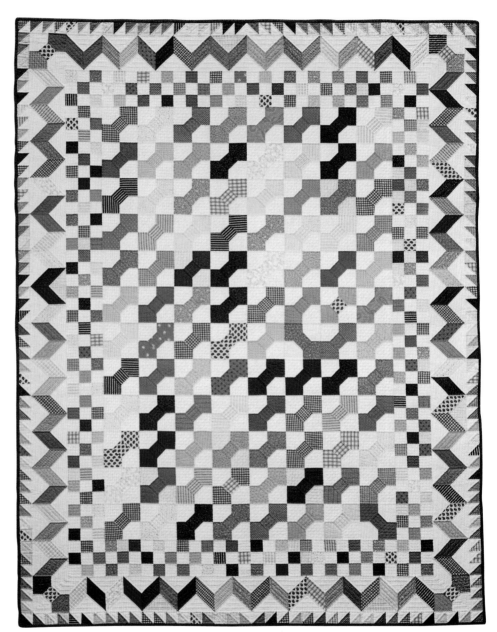

*Homestead Bow Tie*, Heather Waldron Tewell, 76″ × 100″ (193 cm × 254 cm), hand quilted.
The quilting plan grew out of old-fashioned outline quilting. Each of the patches is stitched ¼″ (0.6 cm) inside the seam line. Various straight-line designs, including parallel lines, double parallel lines, on-grain grid, and hanging diamonds, are stitched through each patch to increase the density of the quilting. Staying within each patch emphasizes the seam lines of the quilt top's construction.

*Kobe Lights*, Melody Crust, 18″ × 18″ (45.7 cm × 45.7 cm), machine quilted; private collection.

All nine blocks have white tone-on-tone fabrics as their corner elements. The concentric diamond shapes stitched across the block seams unify these areas of the quilt and downplay how the quilt top was constructed. The spirals across the many patches that make the "lights" pull them into one design unit. Changing thread colors to match the patches from block to block places the emphasis on the shape of the patches and not on the lines created by the stitching. In effect, the quilt has nine "lights" of different colors against a white background.

Designs that cross over seam lines tend to unify those patches into larger elements. If the patches are in adjacent blocks, the quilting will tend to blur the divisions between blocks.

Many pieced blocks and most appliquéd patterns create a motif and a background. Quilting the backgrounds with one design that crosses over seams, and the motifs with another design that also crosses over any seams, is one way to make the motifs stand out from the background. Some pieced blocks create a secondary design: where the four blocks meet, a new design emerges. Quilting the secondary design with its own motif by crossing seams will help to emphasize this second design.

## One Block

Designs that stay within the confines of the block will emphasize the block structure of the quilt and will unify the patches that make up the block. The same design can be stitched on each block, or to add variety to the quilt surface, two or more designs can be alternated across the blocks. When the quilt is set with patterned blocks alternating with plain blocks, one design can be chosen for the pieced or appliquéd block and a different, possibly more complex, one for the plain block.

*The Green Flash*, Melody Crust, 47" × 70" (119.4 cm × 177.8 cm), machine quilted.

The concentric circles, the only design element for the quilting, stay within the block unit. This layout emphasizes the repeat element of the quilt-top design and in this case gives the quilt a rather formal appearance. Notice how the size and placement of the circles create an evenly dense pattern across the quilt surface.

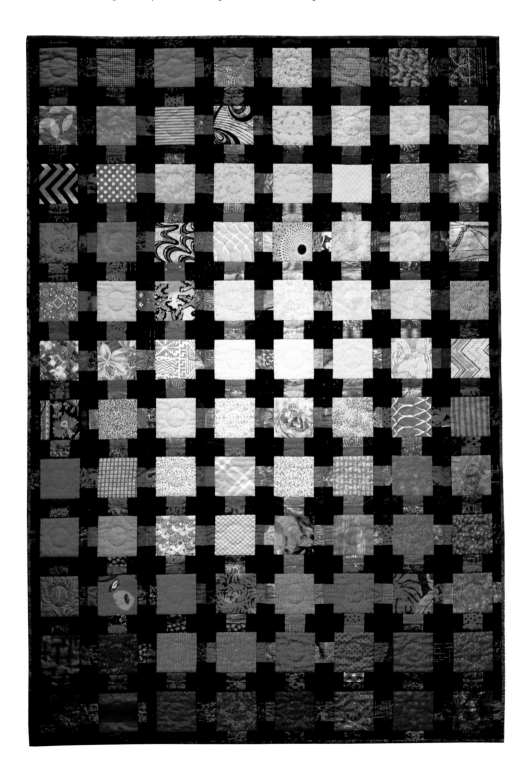

*Spring Churn Dash*, Heather Waldron Tewell, 50″ × 67″ (127 cm × 170.2 cm), hand quilted.

The angular Churn Dash blocks are quilted with two different curved designs. The fabrics in the quilt top are not demanding, being all solids in similar colors of pink. The block design is not complex. For these reasons, this quilt benefited from a greater degree of complexity in the quilting.

*Blue and Brown Churn Dash*, Heather Waldron Tewell, 49″ × 71″ (124.5 cm × 180.3 cm), hand quilted.

The pieced and plain blocks are each stitched with a specific design. The pieced block is hand quilted with simple diagonal lines. The plain block is stitched with a curved floral motif. However, the quilting does not stand out because the fabric is medium-dark and a print.

## The Entire Quilt Surface

The whole quilt top can be the design unit. For example, pioneer quilters stitched fans or hanging diamonds across pieced or appliquéd blocks with total disregard for the seams. Usually, these quilts served a utilitarian function, and the goal was to finish the quilting quickly. Whether or not contemporary quilters have these same objectives, this design solution can be effective. Using one of the old-time quilting designs as an overall pattern will lead to an informal, traditional feeling for the quilt.

When a quilt top consists of large pieces, especially if they are solids, one of the traditional overall designs may give the quilt a utilitarian look. If this is not your intention, increase the complexity of the quilting design, perhaps by adding a shape in the plain areas.

For a quilt top of innovative design, hand and machine quilters alike can invent new overall stitching patterns. Although meander stitching was fresh as machine quilting was coming of age, overuse has limited its appeal as a creative design. For ideas, turn to your design resource book, go to an art museum, or check out your public library's art department. Doodling with pencil on paper can help you approximate stitching lines and can lead to some interesting possibilities.

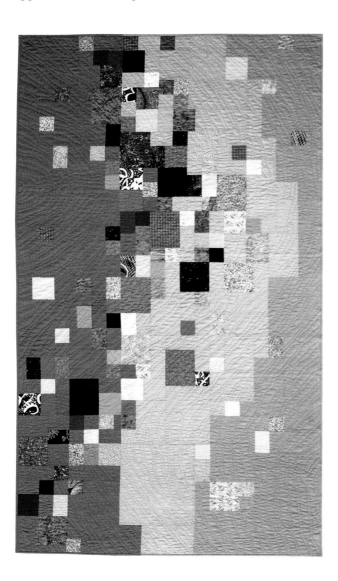

*Beach Rocks*, Heather Waldron Tewell, 40″ × 69″ (101.6 cm × 175.3 cm), hand quilted.

The hand-stitching pattern continues the innovative feeling of the top. The design is intended to suggest ripples on the surface of water and is achieved by stitching elongated ovals side by side. The marks for guiding the stitching were made from the top, using a white chalk pencil, after basting and immediately before each area was stitched.

*Primitive Peony*, Heather Waldron Tewell, 71″ × 71″ (180.3 cm × 180.3 cm), hand quilted.
The old-time quilting pattern called hanging diamonds is used here as an allover design, not as a
background filler. The lines are stitched across the plain muslin areas and continue right over the
appliquéd patches. The only interruptions are the small sunflower elements added for a little interest
in the centers of the large muslin squares.

# Borders

The pattern of the quilting design for the border—whether one strip of fabric, multiple strips, appliquéd elements, or pieced blocks—should coordinate with the quilting designs chosen for the center field of the quilt top. A good approach is to consider repeating a motif already chosen for the center rather than introducing an additional shape or pattern for the border. For example, many traditional quilts use feathered circles in the plain blocks and a feathered wave around the quilt's perimeter. The design taken from the center can be changed in some way to add variety, as when a grid stitched on-grain in the center blocks is changed to a diagonal grid for the border.

Give thought to the complexity, character, and style of the center field's design:

- Is this area already busy with pattern (of fabrics or planned quilting) so that a simple design would provide a balance in the border?
- Is the center rather simple so that an increase in complexity in the border would be welcome to the eye?
- What qualities of line does the center have from the fabrics, piecing, appliqué, or planned quilting: curves, angles, or a combination?
- Would angles, curves, or both best complement the rest of the quilt?
- What style of border pattern will combine well with the overall style of the quilt top and planned quilting in the center field?
- Does the border quilting need to stay traditional?
- Can the border quilting be more innovative but still in keeping with designs already executed or planned?

The idea is to maintain a unity of design among all elements of the quilt, including the borders.

## *One Border or Several Borders*

Adjacent borders can be treated singly or as a unit. For very narrow borders—1½″ (3.8 cm) or less—quilting in the ditch along the seams usually makes the fabric ripple. A better choice is to stitch a simple line or two down the middle or off to one side of the border for a different effect. Wider borders are suitable for more elaborate designs.

Complex designs, like feathered waves, cables, or your original designs, will show best when the fabric is a solid or light-colored print with limited patterning. Remember the maxim If it won't show, keep it simple. Consider simple designs like meanders, grids, and parallel lines when the border fabric is dark or a busy print.

Sometimes, a design is just slightly off—a little too long or a little too short. In this case, each time the stencil or template is repositioned, it can be shifted slightly to take care of the size difference without having to redraft the pattern.

Stitching lines parallel to the quilt's outside edges is one border quilting design that can be particularly problematic. These stitched lines tend to cause excessive rippling. Keeping them parallel to the borders as well as to the outer edge of the quilt can also be difficult. When the lines are perpendicular to the outer edge, the quilt stays flatter.

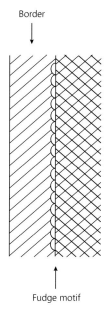

Border

Fudge motif

When adjacent borders or borders next to blocks have similar designs that could be continuous but difficult to mark perfectly, consider placing a fudge motif between them. The introduced motif will interrupt the eye's movement, disguising less-than-precise marking.

*Sherbet*, Heather Waldron Tewell, 50″ × 69″ (127 cm × 175.3 cm), hand quilted. Adjacent borders were treated individually. The narrow lavender border received simple straight lines stitched ¼″ (0.6 cm) inside the seams. This plain design sets off the more complex cable stitched on the wide outer borders.

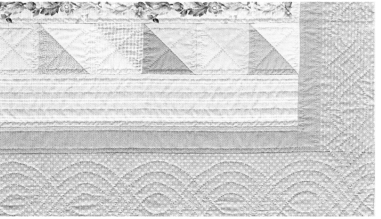

*Gold Fields.*

Lines creating the border design are perpendicular to the sides, not parallel to them. Lines parallel to the sides can be difficult to keep parallel and can cause rippling along the outer edges of the finished quilt. See full quilt on page 55.

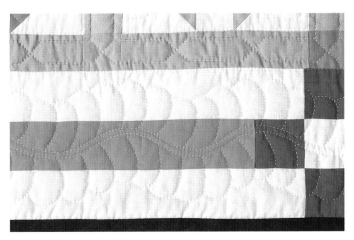

*Spring Churn Dash.*

The strip borders were treated as one unit and quilted with off-white thread. Close up, the thread shows more when it travels across the pink strips than it does across the muslin strips. But when viewed at just a few paces from the quilt, this effect is lost and the design simply reads as a feathered wave. If the wave had been machine stitched instead of hand quilted, perhaps the design choice would not have been as effective. The greater amount of thread laid across the pink strips by the sewing machine would have been visually distracting. See full quilt on page 69.

One design that extends across several borders can be created. This design placement will unify all borders into a frame for the center of the quilt. Be aware when crossing multiple borders that the thread's color and value can make a difference in the visibility of the stitching. If the fabrics making up the border areas contrast and the same color of thread is used overall, the thread may not show equally on all fabrics. This leads to a quilting design that comes and goes. Sometimes, this effect is perfect, but not always.

## Border Corners

The corners of the borders need particular attention; people's eyes naturally go there. If you've chosen a formal style, the quilting designs along the sides need to approach the corners so that they can be turned gracefully with the same design. The border design will contribute to an informal feeling if the corners do not resolve perfectly but simply run into each other. Match the style of the corner treatment to the style of the quilt, formal or informal.

Two common border designs for traditional quilts are feathered waves and cables. Both designs can be given formal or informal corner resolutions. The difficulty with these repeated patterns is to get the corners to work out in the formal manner. Unless the quilt top's construction is carefully planned from the start, the side, top, and bottom borders do not usually divide exactly right. Increasing or decreasing the number of repeats on opposite sides will make the undulations of the feathered wave turn the corners formally. Repositioning, elongating, or shortening the cable repeats will solve the cable design's corner resolution problem.

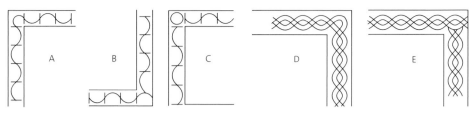

A. A traditional feathered wave looks most formal when the center spines approach the corner in the same way from both directions. All four corners will have the same U-shape resolution, making a continuous wave around the center field.

B. A less formal, more primitive, presentation involves simply running one wave off the edge of the quilt and butting the next one into it. This corner treatment is an alternative to redrafting the wave when informality is desirable and the sides do not come to the corner properly for the U shape.

C. A second possibility for an informal corner resolution is to stop the wave before the corner and insert a feathered circle, feathered heart, or other shape to fill the space.

D. For a cable design to resolve perfectly at the corners, the cables must reach the corners at the same point in the repeated pattern, just like with the feathered wave. The four corners can then be turned with a graceful continuation of all lines.

E. The informal alternative for a cable is to run the design off the edge on one side and butt the other side's design into it.

A. This wave repeats an odd number of times along the ends and an even number of times on the sides. Opposite corners meet in the same way, but all four corners are not the same.

B. One way to make all four corners the same is to change the even repeats to an odd number. Adding one more wave makes the design repeat five times along the long side. Changing the repeat makes a slightly different-looking wave.

C. Another way to change the even repeats to odd is to reduce the number of repeats, here from four to three repeats. The distance between the repeats on the sides was kept the same as the distance between the repeats on the ends so that the waves would be the same shape. The waves on the long sides end short of the corner, but the eye is fooled by the smooth curve.

D. This design solves the even/odd repeat problem by changing the wave pattern in the middle of the long sides. All four corners now resolve perfectly.

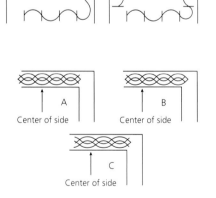

A. To change how the cable reaches the corner, try placing the center of the cable pattern in the center of the side. See how the design comes to the corner.

B. Next, try centering the crossed lines in the center side of the border. See how the design then comes to the corner.

C. A third possibility is to elongate or shorten the cable shape. Here, two repeats of this elongated cable take the design to the corner rather than two and one-half repeats as with the fatter cable.

## Evaluate the Quilt Top

When planning what to quilt, observe the kinds of lines and shapes already present on the quilt top. Generally, pieced designs are angular, while appliquéd patterns are full of curves. Your evaluation should include the lines and shapes in your fabrics as well. Some fabrics, such as florals, read as organic and rounded; others, like stripes and plaids, read as angled or geometric. The same fabric may have both curves and angles.

## Contrast: Curves Versus Angles

After evaluating the character of the lines, shapes, and fabrics of the quilt top, experiment with quilting designs that are the opposite of that character. Very frequently, curved lines will enhance straight piecing or geometric prints. If your quilt is predominantly angular in feeling, play around with cables, circles, feathers, flowers, leaves, or rounded quilting lines of your own creation. The reverse is also true: straight quilting lines will often complement curved appliquéd designs and organic-feeling fabrics. Try concentric squares, diamonds, parallel lines, or some different grid patterns. Contrast in character of line and shape is an effective design tool in quilt making.

On traditional quilts where the pieced or appliquéd design makes a definite motif, such as a LeMoyne Star or a Whig Rose, lines and shapes that contrast with the predominant character of the quilt top allow the pieced or appliquéd design to stand apart from the quilting. Repeating the same kind of line—more curves for the background of an appliquéd top or more angles for a pieced top—can fight with, rather than highlight, the quilt-top design.

The angular background around the star motif and the curves around the flower add little interest because contrast is lacking. Combining curves with angles could create greater visual excitement.

An exception is echo quilting. Echo quilting consists of lines of stitching, by hand or machine, forming concentric rings equidistant from each other around a main motif. Because the stitching follows the contour of the motif, the quilting design will necessarily be the same character as the motif. If the appliquéd design is a curved floral pattern, the quilted lines will follow the curves of the appliqué and have a curved character. If the motif is geometric, the echo quilting will maintain that angular feeling.

Echo quilting is the traditional quilting pattern for Hawaiian-style quilts. If you want to create an authentic-looking Hawaiian quilt, definitely choose echo quilting. Otherwise, echo quilting is simply one of many choices for a background filler design. Audition it as a possibility, but also try a filler design that contrasts in character with your main motif. You decide whether the contrasting design is better or not.

Over the years, a diagonal grid has become the customary choice for the background quilting on traditional appliqué. This is a specific example of the contrast principle at work. Appliqué is usually composed of curves, while the grid design consists of angles. Curves contrast with angles, causing the appliquéd areas to stand out from the background.

In traditional quilt making, a pieced top is frequently quilted with curved shapes. Another application of the contrast principle, this has become standard because it works.

*For My Mother*, Heather Waldron Tewell, 61″ × 77″ (154.9 cm × 195.6 cm), hand quilted; private collection.

The quilting for this curvilinear appliquéd top consists almost entirely of angular designs. Behind the center basket and inner border is a simple diagonal grid. For variety the grid in the outer border around the birds is slightly different, becoming a plaid with double parallel lines in both directions. Small amounts of curved quilting around the birds (meant to suggest wind) add interest without detracting from the focus of the quilt—the appliqué. A simple half circle through each of the appliquéd dogtooth shapes maintains the overall density of the quilting pattern.

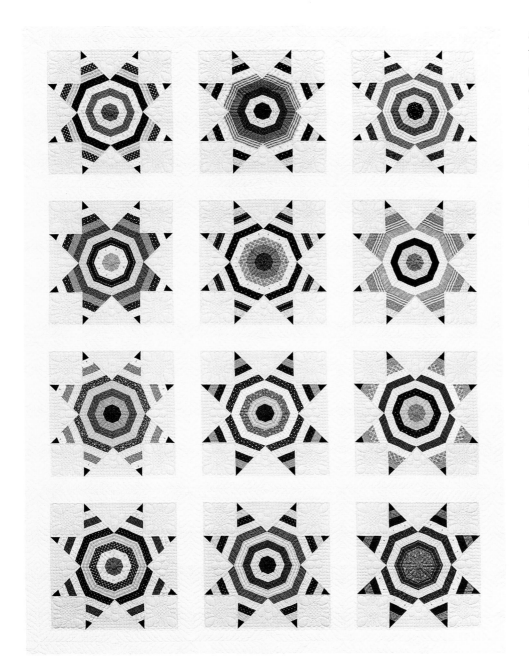

*Marilla's Quilt*, Heather Waldron Tewell, 74" × 97" (188 cm × 246.4 cm), hand quilted.

Quantities of curved feather stitching in the pink and yellow areas balance the bold geometry of the star designs. Notice that the feathered designs fill the patches through which they are stitched to within ¼" (0.6 cm) of the seam lines and that the lines stitched across the pieced stars are evenly dense.

A review of quilting designs on nontraditional quilts shows that they generally mimic the character of the lines and shapes in the quilt top rather than contrast with them. When the surface appears randomly constructed, stitched lines are free-flowing.

When the quilt top is constructed with more geometry, quilting lines are often straighter and more regular. Of course, you can look at any art quilt book or exhibit and find exceptions. But keep these pairings in mind as suggestions for where to start when designing for nontraditional quilts.

Further scrutiny of innovative work shows that more quilts are being stitched with imaginative linear designs than with shapes. This preference may be due to the large number of art quilts that are machine quilted. Because starts and stops are

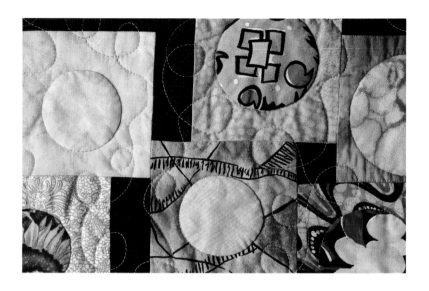

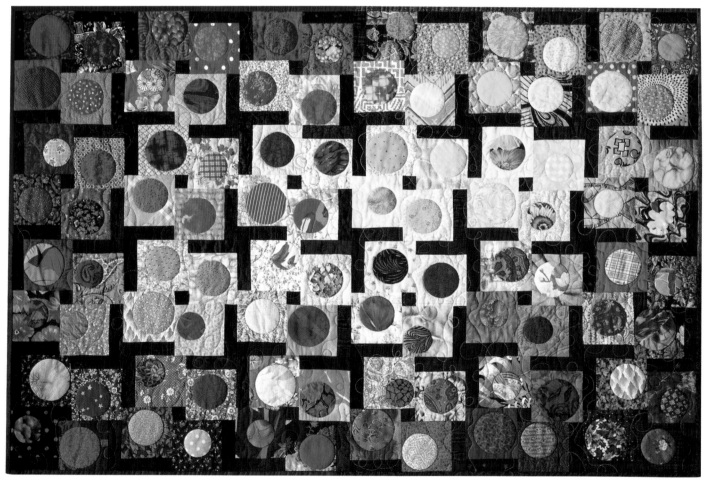

*Champagne*, Melody Crust, 49″ × 33″ (124.5 cm × 83.8 cm), machine quilted.

With appliquéd circles of different sizes and colors bouncing across the surface, the effect of the top's design is one of scattered chaos. The quilting repeats this character. The long looping lines wind around the bubbles with no pattern, frequent changes of direction, and a variety of loop sizes. The stitching purposefully avoids the circles to make them come forward from the background.

*Jacks*, Melody Crust, 57″ × 67″ (144.8 cm × 170.2 cm), machine quilted.

The structure of this quilt is rigidly geometric: square blocks and evenly spaced broken circles in the background and an on-point, square lattice in the foreground. The machine-quilting lines follow the vertical, horizontal, and diagonal lines of the piecing. The art of this quilt is the skillful play on color.

time-consuming by machine, continuous-line designs are preferred over shapes. Even art quilts done by hand tend to use more lines than shapes. Innovators might look on this design gap as an opportunity to do something significant with shapes in their quilting.

## Contrast: Plain Versus Busy Top

In addition to identifying the character of the lines, shapes, and fabrics on a quilt top as angular or rounded, consider the degree of complexity of the pieced or appliquéd design and the variety of colors and patterns in the fabrics.

Simple pieced tops need more elaborate quilting to hold the viewers' interest. Imagine the large areas of solid-colored fabrics used in Amish quilts stitched through the layers with only diagonal parallel lines. People would hardly look twice. Instead, they enjoy the complex combination of baskets, feathers, cables, pumpkin seeds, and grids covering these quilts.

Simple tops are opportunities for elaborate quilting designs. Quilts set with plain squares between pieced or appliquéd blocks usually benefit from quilting that is more complex in the plain areas. The same is true of plain borders. The wider the border, the more it may demand an interesting quilting design to hold the eye.

*Moody Beach*, Heather Waldron Tewell, 45″ × 64″ (114.3 cm × 162.6 cm), machine quilted.

The impact of a quilt with minimal piecing such as this one depends on the beauty and complexity of the quilting design.

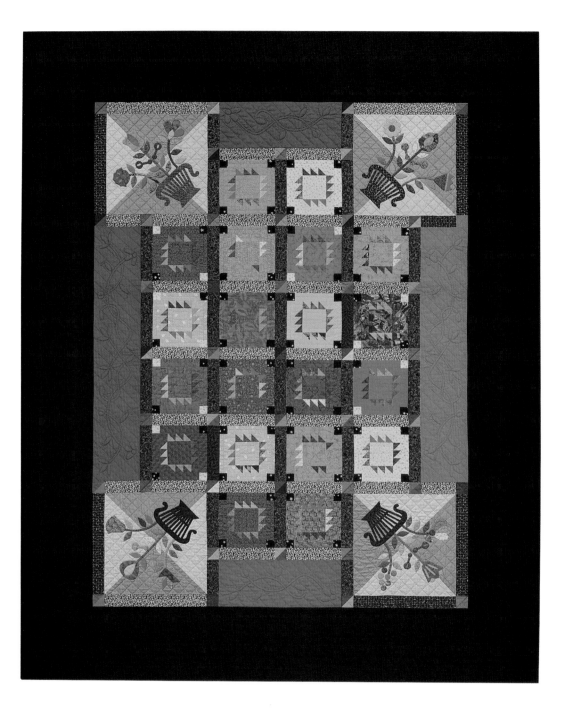

*Nightshades*, Heather Waldron Tewell, 64″ × 80″ (162.6 cm × 203.2 cm), hand quilted; private collection.

The wide outer border is quilted with simple diagonal lines. The only variation is a change of direction at the midpoint of each side. The center field is very busy with vivid color, different patterned fabrics, both piecing and appliqué, areas of trapunto in the solid red rectangles, and many small patches within the block units. An elaborate quilting design in the outer border would fight with, rather than enhance, the quilt top. The quiet border allows the focus to remain in the center field of the quilt.

Conversely, when the piecing or appliqué is very busy or there is a great variety of colors and patterns in the fabrics chosen, simple quilting may be all that is required. Outline stitching, parallel lines, or a grid will hold the three layers together without competing with the quilt top's own design.

Whether a simple or complex quilting pattern is needed depends upon the degree of complexity of the quilt surface coupled with your own design sense. Some people are comfortable with a lot of busy patterns while others tolerate much less. Work with your quilting design, auditioning a range of patterns from simple to complex until you are satisfied.

# Repetition as a Design Tool

The design goal of the quilting is to create a pattern that complements the quilt top's design. Another way to think about this is to strive for some relationship—a unity of design—between the quilt top and the quilting.

Repetition, a tool well known to people creating in all kinds of disciplines, works amazingly well as a design guide for quilting both traditional and nontraditional quilts. The repeated element can be

- a line
- a shape
- a theme

This element can be found in

- the pieced or appliquéd design
- the fabrics
- the theme itself

## *Repetition of Shape: Outlining*

The classic example of repetition is outline quilting. On a pieced top, outlining is usually done ¼" (0.6 cm) inside a patch, repeating the shape of the patch. No marking is required, which saves time and has made this design a popular choice.

Outlining alone may be enough quilting when individual patches are uniformly small. From a design standpoint, if the pieced quilt surface is already very busy with many prints, value changes, and wide-ranging colors, a quiet quilting design like outlining can be ideal.

When more quilting is needed, outlining can be combined with filler lines or shapes inside the patches to increase the density of the quilting and to add visual interest. Fillers can be simple, like a diagonal line, or more complex, like a daisy centered on a square. They can be curved like a circle or angular like a five-pointed star. The filler design you choose will depend upon whether curves or angles complement your top design and how much quilting needs to be added to carry the visual weight of the quilt top.

Sometimes, shapes can be converted to continuous lines for machine quilting by connecting stitching across seams and yet still give the feeling of repeated shapes.

Lone Star can be stitched easily by machine with continuous lines using the walking foot or even-feed feature.

For example, on a Lone Star, you turn diamond shapes into a diamond grid by stitching long lines on either side of the seams. Here is a place where machine quilting has an advantage over hand quilting: the machine crosses all those seams easily.

## Repetition of Patterns from the Quilt Top

Shapes formed by the piecing or used in the appliqué can become an element of the quilting design. In the case of piecing, the repeated element is the shape of the larger design created by the individual pieces. With Grandmother's Flower Garden again as the example, concentric circles, either round or following the shifting angles of the hexagons, can be used as the quilting design. On an Ohio Star block, the star can be outline quilted to create a design element. In the case of appliqué, the shape of one or more of the appliquéd patches can be repeated as a quilting motif.

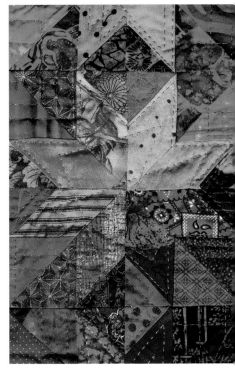

*Starz*, Melody Crust, 24″ × 31″ (61 cm × 78.7 cm), machine quilted; private collection.
Outline stitching repeats the star shape in the piecing. Overlapping triangles, suggesting additional star points, fill in the star centers.

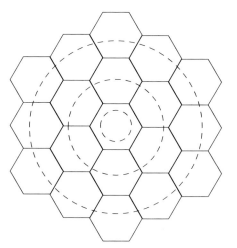
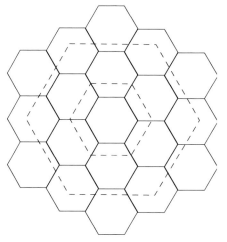
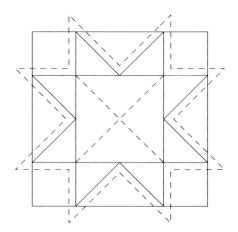

For Grandmother's Flower Garden, concentric circles or concentric hexagons as the quilting design come directly from the repetition of the patches.

The star of an Ohio Star block can be outlined. Additional lines, such as the X in the star's center, will be needed so that the quilting is evenly distributed across the surface.

Whether on a pieced or appliquéd quilt, these shape designs will likely need to be paired with a background filler or additional motifs to complete the entire quilting design.

## Repetition of Theme

Representational quilts—those with some realism to the quilt top's pieced or appliquéd design—are tailor-made for using the quilt top's theme as a springboard to the quilting design. The shape of the appliqué itself can simply be repeated. For

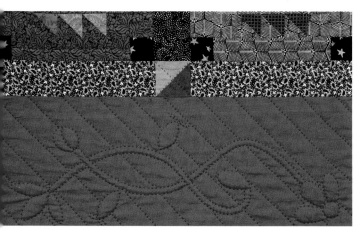

*Nightshades.*

The shapes creating the stuffed work design were taken directly from the corner appliquéd blocks. This complex quilting pattern was stitched where it would show: on plain fabrics. In the center pieced area where the colors vary widely, the piecing is dense, and the fabrics are patterned, the quilting design is simply straight lines. See full quilt on page 83.

*Rose Wreath.*

The floral quilting design in the border repeats elements from the appliquéd patches but in a running-vine arrangement. The grid used as background filler varies from inside to outside the wreaths, giving subtle definition to these areas. Inside the wreath the grid is close and placed on the straight of the fabric. Surrounding the wreath the grid is wider and on the diagonal. See full quilt on page 54.

example, a flower motif from the appliqué can be used again for the quilting design in a plain area. Rather than repeating the shape as it appears on the quilt top, think about using a detail from within the thematic idea.

The theme that is repeated can come from the design of the fabric used in the quilt. The design elements in the fabric can be outlined, or the thematic motifs can be scattered over the surface without regard to the placement of the motifs on the fabric. In either case, filler lines should be included as needed to give a uniform density to the quilting. For example, perhaps the quilt uses star fabrics in many shapes and sizes. Star motifs could be repeated shapes for the quilting design. Stars could also be outline stitched exactly as seen on the fabric (consider the size of the motif

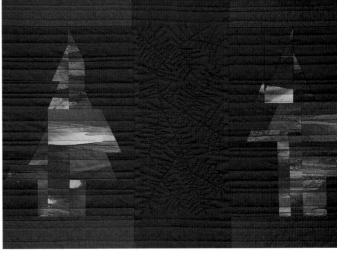

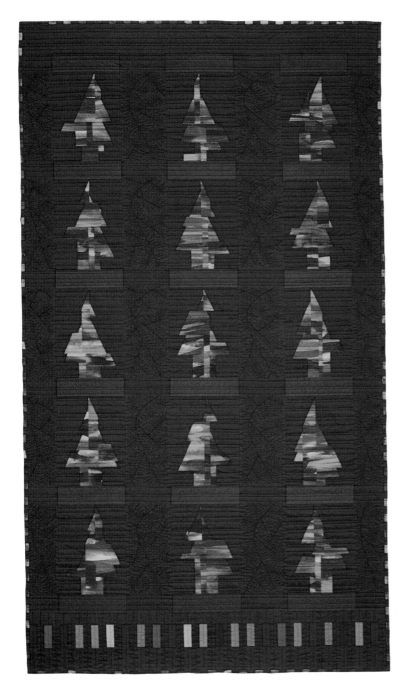

*Conifers Across the Bay*, Heather Waldron Tewell, 47″ × 86″ (119.4 cm × 218.4 cm), machine quilted.
The pieced Douglas fir trees are small, nowhere near the 100′ (30.5 m) size of a real tree. On the other hand, the machine-stitched boughs in the plain blocks are life-size. The quilting design uses a tree theme but with a change in scale between the pieced pattern and the quilted motif. A quiet design of irregularly spaced lines stitched across the pieced trees keeps the focus of the quilting on the plain blocks.

*Urban Oasis*, Melody Crust, 36″ × 48″
(91.4 cm × 121.9 cm), machine quilted;
private collection.

The idea for the machine quilting came
from the fabrics. The shapes of the trees,
flowers, and leaves are repeated through
outline stitching. For density as well as
realism purposes, more garden elements
were added: flowers, leaves, and grass. A
flowing stitched line fills the sky area.

when thinking about this option). However, the design might be more interesting if the star shapes were stitched without regard to where stars appear on the fabric.

Another idea is to select a whole-cloth backing fabric that coordinates with the theme of the front and has a pattern that can be adapted for stitching. The quilt can be machine stitched with the backing fabric facing up so that the pattern on the fabric can be followed. The bobbin thread makes the design on the front of the quilt. For example, a quilt top in light and dark shades of purple floral fabrics pieced into a Log Cabin design might have a fabric with large flowers for the backing. The floral design of the backing fabric repeats the floral theme in the quilt top. Using free motion and stitching on the quilt upside down (the backing is on the top), you can outline stitch individual flowers with variegated purple thread in the bobbin. When the stitching is completed, thread outlines of flowers will appear on the front of the quilt.

## Combination of Design Motifs

Before you begin to stitch, evaluate your design plan for the proposed combinations of patterns.

Be wary of using too many different design motifs. Quilters are easily tempted to include many beautiful traditional designs or to use many linear designs that they have invented for continuous machine stitching—all on the same quilt. Often, a more integrated design comes from repeating or varying one of the designs rather than choosing a different motif from a totally different family of designs.

Your evaluation can lead to the opposite conclusion as well. Perhaps more variety would be beneficial for the particular quilt top and the quilting design planned. Creating more complexity in just one portion of the design may be all that is needed. For example, if the same background filler pattern is proposed throughout the quilt, consider changing an area—perhaps the outer border—to a similar but slightly different pattern.

## In Review

No doubt, as quilt making continues to evolve in the twenty-first century, quilters will be using exciting new techniques and different materials that will add challenge and fascination to the expanding repertoire of quilting design. The exercises that follow will help you dissect a quilt into its various elements and will give you practice with free-motion and machine stitching.

1.  Examine quilts to see how other quilters are combining lines and shapes. Do you see lines going diagonally, horizontally, or vertically? Do you see shapes—hearts, suns, moons, flowers? Look in a book of quilting designs and see which shapes attract you. Trace or draw them, and put them in your design notebook.

2.  To improve your free-motion technique, create a sample quilt sandwich and practice stitching the design you drew for the meander designs exercise in Chapter Three. Then, to really advance your free-motion stitching, create a continuous or semi-continuous design and stitch it on one of your quilt tops. Give yourself permission to keep going in spite of broken threads and jerky lines. By the time you have finished stitching the entire quilt, your ability to control stitch length and direction will have improved and you will be better able to handle the bulk of the quilt. Consider practicing on a community service quilt.

3.  To see what stitching effects might be possible with your machine, create a sample quilt sandwich and stitch it with different programmed stitches: serpentine, zigzag, and satin stitch—try others, too. Vary the stitch lengths and widths to see what effects you can achieve. Record your work in your design notebook.

4.  Go through your quilt magazines, books, and photographs, focusing on borders. What has the quilt maker done to make the border quilting design relate to the center field's design? Photocopy any interesting treatments, and place them in your design notebook.

To minimize bulk, flatten the quilt, and reduce skipped stitches when machine quilting, iron open the seams of the quilt top and the back wherever possible. You will not be able to stitch in the ditch along seams that have been pressed open.

A traditional feather motif can be designed to fill the rectangular block with a simple hanging-diamonds pattern for the yellow centers. To maintain the uniform density of stitching across the quilt, some quilting needs to be in the brown sashing. One line down the center of these strips would do, but using two lines in the vertical sashing and one in the horizontal might be more interesting. This quilting pattern emphasizes the repeated-block construction while introducing the complexity of multiple curves to complement the angular piecing.

The color scheme and suggestion of layered brown and turquoise grids provide the visual impact for this quilt top. Lines in the piecing are crisply straight. The patches are rectangles in various sizes, except for the strips of sashing. The colors, while vivid, are limited: slight variations in fuchsia, yellow, and turquoise, with the brown as a neutral. An evaluation of the fabrics and pieced pattern in the top leads to the conclusion that the top is a simple pieced design and therefore an ideal candidate for more complex quilting.

Several options for placement of quilting designs are apparent. A stitching pattern can be created that reinforces the block. Another possibility is to center a design motif on the intersections of the sashing strips. This quilting pattern will emphasize the layered brown and turquoise lattices.

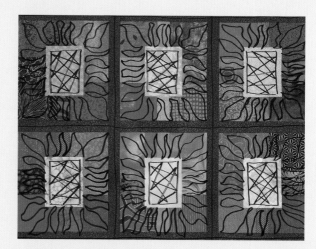

This variation of the feathered rectangle repeats within the block unit. Because each design is unique and the lines are squiggly, the pattern adds great dynamic interest to the quilt surface. A machine quilter might use rayon or metallic thread to push the quilt further toward a non-traditional look.

The hanging-diamonds pattern of the previous sketch has been converted to a continuous-line design easily stitched by machine but also possible by hand.

This quilting pattern blurs the block construction. The curved floral shapes, centered on the intersections of the sashing, shift the emphasis. The vertical lines, which are boxy in contrast to the curves of the neighboring designs, increase in complexity as they cross the yellow rectangles. Straight lines through the horizontal turquoise patches complete the design. This placement of quilting motifs creates the effect of overlapping lattices, leaving the viewer to decide which is on top and which is behind. The quilt achieves a formal elegance.

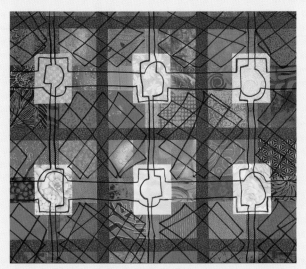

This sketch was an experiment. Sometimes an idea is better in the mind than in reality, but it is always worth testing. The concept was to trade places with the curves and the angles in the previous design. However, the boxy lines centered on the brown sashing intersections achieve only a flat and functional feeling. Lines across the yellow rectangles do not read like shapes; they just seem messy. Neither area is as appealing as in the last quilting plan. Sometimes, you cannot know about a design until you see it.

*Red Hot*, Melody Crust and Heather Waldron Tewell, 23" × 35" (58.4 cm × 88.9 cm), machine quilted.

The flame-shaped quilting design, following the sketch on the bottom right of page 90, carries out the hot fire theme. Two different patterns drawn onto tear-away paper and used at random increase the complexity of the fires. The sashing rippled when stitched with a simple line down the center, so in-the-ditch stitching was added. Threads of different fibers and colors—silk, rayon, and cotton in red and yellow—give subtle visual interest.

# CHAPTER SIX

# Batting, Backing, and Thread

THE PATTERNS OF LINES and shapes stitched through the layers by hand or machine, together with the design of the quilt top, have the most obvious impact on the beauty and success of a finished quilt. Less obvious but still influential components are the supporting cast of batting, backing, and thread. These materials can affect the look of a completed quilt tremendously. The variety in each category is great. Understanding the technical properties and design considerations surrounding batting, backing, and thread will help you to make informed selections that, in turn, will help you achieve the quilt you envision.

Christine Falls on Van Trump Creek, Mount Rainier National Park, Washington. The beauty of an object can be enhanced by its surroundings. Observers respond to this waterfall because they see it against a pleasurable background—pristine nature and an historic bridge. When choosing the backing for a quilt, think of the whole picture, and choose a fabric or fabrics that relate to the quilt top's design. You may be surprised at the increased pleasure this will give you or the new owner as the quilt is handled over the years. Leaves, rocks, falling water, and stone bridges are wonderful inspirations for the quilting design.

# Batting

The subject of batting, more than any other area of quilt making, is a maze. The puzzle gets more complicated every year as manufacturers add new products. Very few quilters have the time or inclination, let alone financial resources, to test every batting on the market.

Battings can be evaluated for a long list of properties:

- fiber content
- feel
- drape
- look
- breathability
- shrinkage
- opaqueness
- ease of stitching
- closeness of stitching required
- tendency to beard
- thickness

## *Fiber Content*

Batting can be divided into two large categories based on fiber content: (1) natural fibers such as cotton, silk, and wool; and (2) synthetic fibers, largely polyester. Blends of cotton and polyester, usually 80 percent cotton and 20 percent polyester, are also available.

Machine quilters generally prefer cotton and cotton/polyester-blended battings. Cotton battings stick to the cotton in the fabrics of the quilt top and backing. This gripping action augments pin basting, reducing the likelihood of puckers being stitched into the quilt. Cotton and cotton/polyester battings also hang well. For these reasons, machine and hand quilters alike prefer cotton and cotton blends for their wall hangings.

If you are hand stitching a bed-size quilt in a hoop, a polyester batting is a good choice. The polyester batting will not be as heavy as a similar-sized cotton batting, reducing the strain on your body during the stitching process.

## *Feel*

As with many issues in the selection of a quilt batting, the feel of the batting (what it is like to handle a quilt made with a particular batting) is subjective. Purists will say that nothing feels as good as 100 percent cotton. Cotton has a density to it that makes it pleasant to handle. However, blended battings (80 percent cotton/20 percent polyester) tend to feel and behave like 100 percent cotton battings. Others who prefer lighter bedding appreciate the weightless, thinner feel of polyester, silk, or wool.

| Category of Batting | Specific Characteristics | Uses |
| --- | --- | --- |
| 100 percent cotton | Breathes<br>Shrinks; preshrink only if manufacturer's directions allow<br>Does not catch fire easily; does not melt<br>Minimal bearding<br>Drapes well; be careful of grain<br>Little or no shadowing through<br>Quilting lines can be spaced a maximum of 1" (2.5 cm) apart; sometimes closer spacing is required<br>Needling takes skill | Can give puckered look of antique quilts<br>Good for bedding |
| Needle-punched 100 percent cotton | Breathes<br>Hangs without distortion; no grain<br>Minimal bearding<br>Opaque<br>Quilting lines can be spaced a maximum of 8" (20.3 cm) apart<br>May be preshrunk<br>Can be too thick for hand quilting | Machine quilting<br>Especially good for machine-quilted wall hangings<br>Stands up well to heavy use |
| 80 percent cotton/ 20 percent polyester blends | Quilting lines can be spaced a maximum of 2" (5.1 cm) to 3" (7.6 cm) apart<br>Drapes well<br>May be prewashed | When the feel and drape of cotton batting are desired without close quilting required by 100 percent cotton battings |
| Wool | Quilting lines can be spaced a maximum of 3" (7.6 cm) apart<br>Warm without weight<br>Extra care necessary when laundering<br>To avoid bearding, choose resinated wool<br>More expensive than other battings | Warm, lightweight bedding<br>When tiny stitches in hand quilting are important |
| Silk | Not available in a wide variety of sizes<br>Quilting lines can be spaced a maximum of 1½" (3.8 cm) apart<br>Easy to needle<br>Lightweight<br>Drapes well | Clothing |
| Polyester | Quilting lines can be spaced a maximum of 2" (5.1 cm) to 3" (7.6 cm) apart<br>Warm without weight but does not breathe<br>Melts in excessive heat<br>May lose loft with many washings | Large bed coverings<br>When tiny stitches in hand quilting are important |

## Drape

"Drape" refers to the way a quilt either hangs on the wall or drops from the sides of a bed. Over long distances, cotton battings and blends hang the best because they have good weight. Polyester battings specially manufactured to have long, vertical fibers (originally intended for use in garments where drape is especially important) also hang well. Silk battings drape beautifully.

The amount of quilting also affects drape. The thicker the quilt batting, the stiffer a quilt tends to become when densely stitched, especially when machine quilted.

Some battings have grain created in the manufacturing process, just like fabric. These battings hang best when the length of the batting is placed vertically, thus bearing the weight of gravity.

## Look, Loft, and Shrinkage

"Loft" refers to how much the batting puffs after quilting. Some battings give a quilt a very flat appearance, almost as if nothing is between the layers. These battings tend to be thin and 100 percent cotton. Other battings are all puff, giving a quilt a very sculpted appearance. The fluffiest battings are high-loft polyester; often these are reserved for tied comforters. The majority of battings present a medium relief when quilted.

The look of a batting is also affected by the amount it shrinks after washing. One hundred percent cotton battings and cotton/polyester battings can shrink as much as 5 percent. Some quilters want the puckered look of an old quilt and will purposefully wait to shrink a batting until after the quilting is finished. If the puckered look is not desired, preshrinking the batting following the manufacturer's recommended directions will result in a flatter quilt. Remember to allow for shrinkage when purchasing your batting.

Some battings will not shrink. Polyester and silk battings do not shrink, nor will wool battings if washed according to the manufacturer's instructions.

## Breathability

"Breathability" is the ease with which air flows through a batting. When a quilt is intended to keep someone warm rather than hang on a wall, it is important to realize that airflow through the batting fibers will increase the comfort of the quilt. Cotton, wool, and silk fibers trap air, but they also allow excess warmth to flow out. Polyester battings, like polyester clothes, trap and also retain air, making the bedding warmer than some people find comfortable.

## Opaqueness and Shadowing Through

"Opaqueness" refers to the see-through quality of a batting. The degree of opaqueness depends upon thickness as well as the fiber from which the batting is made. Cotton battings are the most opaque. Polyester fibers of any thickness can be seen through much more easily than cotton fibers of equal thickness. However, the thickest polyester battings approach the opaque quality of cotton.

## Techniques

**Prewashing** Prewashing can be tricky. Some manufacturers advise against prewashing their battings because the substance holding the fibers in place will wash away. If this kind of batting is washed before the fibers are held in place by quilting stitches, the batting will be ruined. Other manufacturers do not recommend prewashing a batting because quilters' handling techniques are uneven. Without great care, lifting a batting when it is full of water or wringing to expel water can cause distortion or tears in the batting. These manufacturers prefer to avoid all problems by telling quilters not to prewash. The best solution is to read the manufacturer's directions and follow them carefully when prewashing is allowed. If you have questions, contact the manufacturer.

**Shrinkage from the Quilting** When a quilt requires a particular finished size, such as when the quilt is intended for a specific bed or space on the wall, consideration must be given to shrinkage that occurs simply from the quilting. Whether a piece is hand or machine quilted, the more stitching there is, the more effect the stitching will have on the finished size of the quilt. On a large bed-size quilt the shrinkage can be as much as 2" (5.1 cm) in both width and length. One possible solution, heavily dependent on the design of the quilt, is to add some extra width to the outer border. Before the binding is applied, the quilt can be cut to the desired size. Of course, not all quilts have plain borders and many have no borders at all. In these cases, the best practice is to design the top a little bigger overall to allow for some shrinkage.

The opaqueness of a batting is important when the quilt top is constructed in whole or in part from light fabrics. If the backing fabrics are dark, or have great contrast in patterning from light to dark, and the batting is not opaque, the dark portions of the backing will change the color of the light parts of the quilt top. To preserve the beauty of the quilt's surface, the backing should not show through to the front of the quilt. This phenomenon is called shadowing through. A white cotton batting will keep the light-colored fabrics in a quilt top looking crisp.

Suppose a quilt top consists of blocks in a navy blue star pattern with white fabrics for the background of the stars. The blocks are set with alternate plain blocks that are also white. To carry out the theme, a backing fabric is proposed that has brightly colored stars in deep red scattered across a white background. The batting being considered is a medium-weight polyester. Where white fabric on the front of the quilt rests on top of white background on the backing fabric, there will be no problem. But where the backing's bright stars are behind the white fabric on the quilt top, shadows of the stars will likely be visible through the batting.

Two solutions are possible:

1. Choose a light-colored backing with less value contrast between the design motif and the background.
2. Select a batting that is opaque, such as one of the cotton or cotton-blend battings.

The backing fabrics for this block are pieced vertically down the middle. The left half is a navy blue fabric; the right half is a white fabric. The batting is polyester. Notice the dulling effect on the white fabrics where the dark backing shadows through.

### Ease of Stitching or Needling

For machine quilters, ease of needling is not an issue. The machine does the work and will make perfect stitches through all kinds and thicknesses of batting when the size of the needle is matched to both the thread and thickness of the sandwich.

For hand quilters seeking to make tiny stitches, ease of stitching has primary importance.

Generally, polyester, silk, and wool are easier to needle than cotton or cotton/polyester blends. These battings are easier because fewer fibers are needed in

The prevention of fiber migration is not the only technical function of the quilting stitches. When a quilt is handled and especially when it is washed, adequate quilting ensures that quilting threads will not break. A wet quilt can be very heavy; the weight will pop stitches unless the lines of quilting are close enough to provide support. The farther apart the lines of quilting are, the stronger the thread needs to be. Conversely, the denser the stitching pattern, the lighter the thread can be. When in doubt, choose a heavier thread or stitch lines closer together.

a given space to give loft; the fibers themselves have a natural springy quality. These fewer fibers can be condensed into a small space on the quilting needle. Cotton and cotton/polyester blends require more fibers to make the same amount of loft, and the fibers themselves are thicker. Simply as a matter of physical properties, more pressure is needed to condense the cotton fibers onto the quilting needle, making cotton slightly more difficult to needle.

## Closeness of Stitching Required

The spacing of quilting lines depends on a combination of the function of the quilt, the fiber content of the batting, and how the batting was manufactured. The purpose of the quilting is to hold the batting in place during use of the quilt. Without adequate stitching, batting fibers tend to migrate, forming lumps. Some fibers tend to lump more than others. Fiber migration results in a quilt that is less warm; where the fibers have withdrawn, there are only two layers and no insulating value from the batting. This condition also makes a quilt less pleasing to look at and handle.

In the early days when 100 percent cotton batting was spread evenly over the quilt surface by hand, quilting as closely as ¼″ (0.6 cm) to ½″ (1.3 cm) was required or the quilt would become lumpy. Today, batting manufacturers have invented processes and are using materials purposely to control fiber migration. See the discussion of fiber migration in Chapter Two.

Manufacturers have done tests to determine how close lines of stitching need to be on their battings to prevent fiber migration. The manufacturer's recommended-spacing labels on batting products state this number. For example, when a manufacturer says, "This batting can be stitched up to ten inches apart," no fiber migration should occur on a quilt made from this product when it is stitched with a checkerboard 10″ (25.4 cm) wide. Another label might read "two-inch spacing required." This batting needs quilting as close as every 2″ (5.1 cm) in order to avoid fiber migration.

These numbers assume that a quilt is going to be washed and used. If the quilt will be a wall hanging that will never be washed, the manufacturer's recommended spacing can be ignored, and the quilting need only be what your eye says complements the quilt top. In many cases, this quilting will be as close as or closer than the manufacturer's recommended spacing to prevent sagging of the fabrics in the quilt top and to create an effective stitching pattern.

## Bearding

"Bearding" refers to the action of batting fibers traveling through to the front or back surface of a quilt. It is often confused with migrating, which occurs when the handling of a quilt causes fibers to mat together inside the quilt sandwich. Bearding is undesirable because it leaves fuzzy fibers on the quilt's surface, which are unsightly and unpleasant, like lint on a business suit. As more and more fibers separate from the batting, the quilt's insulating value can be reduced substantially.

Bearding seems to be affected by the kinds of fabrics used in a quilt. Some combinations of batting and fabrics result in bearding and some do not. Unfortunately, there is no way to know for sure whether or not a batting will beard. Thankfully, bearding does not happen very often.

*Dungeness in the Eelgrass*, Heather Waldron Tewell, 46″ × 78″ (116.8 cm × 198.1 cm), hand quilted. This quilt was originally hand basted using a cotton batting between the layers. Even as the basting was in progress, significant numbers of batting fibers pulled through to the front of the quilt. Perhaps this bearding was due to the batik fabrics of the quilt top. When a long-fiber polyester batting was substituted for the cotton batting, the bearding ceased and did not reappear during quilting.

## Thickness

Battings come in an array of thicknesses. Generally, the thinner the batting, the flatter the finished quilt will be, the less warm it will be, and the easier it will be to needle by hand. Very thick or high-loft batting is best for tying. In between are various medium weights.

## Selecting the Right Batting

The batting you choose should depend upon careful balancing of the pros and cons of the characteristics in each batting under consideration. The same batting will not necessarily be the best choice for every project. Major factors to consider are

- whether you intend to quilt by hand or by machine
- how much time you can devote to the stitching (some battings require denser stitching than others)
- your preference for particular fibers
- the quilt's function (wall hanging or bed covering)

Experience with batting is the best and possibly only real teacher. Read all you can about the various products, talk with experienced quilt makers, and make your best selection based on this information. Then begin a log of your experiences. At a minimum, record the batting used in every quilt either in a card file, on your computer, or on the label of the quilt itself. You will have an even more useful set of data if you

## Options

A few scenarios may clarify the batting decision.

**Scenario 1** Linda's project is a wall hanging for her mother. She plans to quilt it by machine. Linda will want a batting with good drape and adequate weight so that it will hang well. She will want the batting to cling to her cotton fabrics during the basting and stitching process to make machine quilting easier. The batting should not require close quilting, because she doesn't have time. Recommendation: a needle-punched cotton or cotton/polyester-blend batting. Cotton and cotton blends drape well and have good weight. The needle-punching process stabilizes the fibers, reducing the density of stitching required.

**Scenario 2** Debbie prefers to hand quilt; tiny, even stitches are important to her. The quilt top she has just completed is quite large; when finished, it will be used on her daughter's bed. Debbie will want to choose a thin batting in order to make perfect stitches. She can use a thin cotton; however, she will likely be

able to create smaller stitches using a regular-weight polyester batting. Polyester may have other advantages. The polyester batting will make a warmer bed covering. And, assuming Debbie quilts in a hoop and not a floor frame, the weight of the quilt will be less as she maneuvers the quilt in and out of the hoop, reducing strain on her body during the quilting process.

**Scenario 3** Kathy is working on a baby quilt. She knows that this quilt will be washed frequently and will not last forever. Her plan is to do the long lines of stitching on the machine with a walking foot and some fancy quilting by hand. Kathy will want to choose an 80 percent cotton/20 percent polyester batting. The cotton content will cause the batting to stick to the cotton fabrics in the quilt top, easing her way in machine stitching. While not as easy to stitch by hand as polyester, cotton/polyester blends are relatively easy to needle and generally do not require as close quilting as a 100 percent cotton batting. Thus, Kathy will not have to do a supreme amount of quilting on a project that will be worn out in a few years.

include characteristics of the batting in your file. With this record you can repeat a batting selection that worked well for you.

# Backing

The backing fabric should be 4″ (10.2 cm) to 6″ (15.2 cm) wider and 4″ (10.2 cm) to 6″ (15.2 cm) longer than the quilt top. The extra backing fabric is folded over the batting and the edges of the quilt during the final step in basting. It protects both the batting and the edges of the quilt while you're quilting. The basting process is fully explained in Chapter Seven.

Although the back of a quilt will not show to the casual observer of either a bed quilt or a wall hanging, the entire quilt—front and back—is enjoyed by the maker and the owner. Selecting fabric for the back that relates to the quilt top will increase the pleasure of handling and use of the finished quilt. The relationship can come from repetition: repeat the colors in the quilt top, repeat the motifs in the fabrics, or repeat the theme. For example, a quilt top pieced in a tree pattern could have shades of green for the backing fabric, fabrics with tree images, or fabrics with birds, since birds sit in trees.

*Stone Wall Impression #1.*

In addition to using repetition as a unifying element for the quilt back and front, another idea would be to add some element on the back that is withheld from the front. Here, the front consists of black-and-white fabrics only, no color. For the back, black-and-white fabrics that also have bright colors surprise the eye as the quilt is handled. See full quilt on page 11.

## Fabric Selection

Backing fabric should be 100 percent cotton of good quality. Putting low-quality, inexpensive fabric on the back may save money, but it will definitely shorten the life of the quilt.

In spite of the fact that bedsheets come in wider widths than regular yard goods, sheeting is not recommended as the backing of a quilt to be hand quilted. The thread count is substantially higher than regular cotton fabrics, making it difficult to achieve small stitches. Many fabric stores carry extra-wide 100 percent cotton fabric for those who do not want to have seams on the backs of their quilts.

The depth of color of the backing fabric is an important consideration when light-colored fabrics are present in the quilt top and a see-through batting like polyester has been selected. Dark backing fabric can shadow through to the front. Do a test layering of the proposed backing fabric with the batting and quilt top to see if a shadow-through problem exists. If it does, switch to a lighter-colored backing fabric or a more opaque batting.

Patterned fabric is a good choice for the back of a quilt. Busy prints camouflage less-than-perfect stitches created by hand or machine. Once again, be aware of the potential shadow-through problem. Many prints have high value contrast that could show through to the quilt top.

## Piecing

Frequently, the back of a quilt must be pieced in order to achieve the necessary size. Avoid placing a seam down the middle of the back either horizontally or vertically. People habitually fold down the center first. This folding, repeated in the same place, will weaken the seam. Depending upon the size needed, the backing can be pieced by adding a length either down each side or just along one side.

In the days when all stitching was done by hand, seam allowances were pressed to one side to give the seam added strength. Today, sewing machines create strong seams, and the available threads are strong. The reason to press seams to one side no longer exists. In fact, a case for pressing seams open can be made. Open seams spread out the bulk of the seam allowance. For machine quilters, this practice means fewer skipped

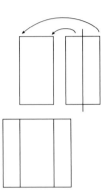

When you need a wider backing and desire minimal piecing, use fabric twice the length of the quilt top plus at least 12" (30.5 cm). The extra inches are protection for the outer edges of the quilt top during the quilting process. Assuming the backing needs to be two widths of the fabric, cut the fabric into equal lengths and split one of these vertically (parallel to the selvages) into two. Sew one of the split widths to either side of the uncut piece.

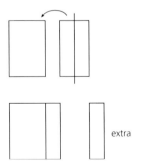

extra

If the quilt backing does not need the double width of the fabric, the back can be pieced with just one vertical seam placed off center.

When preparing the quilt sandwich for basting, make sure the seams in the backing do not line up with the long seams in the quilt top. Short seams like those creating the quilt blocks usually cannot be avoided, but long seams like those in the sashing strips can. Offsetting seams will make quilting go more smoothly for both hand and machine stitchers.

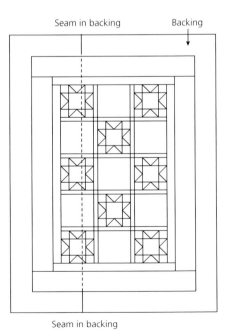

Seam in backing          Backing

Seam in backing

*Star Bright*, Melody Crust, 60″ × 60″ (152.4 cm × 152.4 cm), machine quilted; private collection. The leftover bits from the quilt top's construction were sewn into the back. This back was so much fun to sew that all the bits were used. Another block had to be created for the label.

stitches caused by sewing through uneven thickness. For hand quilters, open seams mean even, tiny stitches can continue across seams more successfully because the difference in thickness from seam allowance to no seam allowance is not as great.

Be careful to offset the seams on the backing with any long, continuous seams on the front of the quilt. Offsetting seams is another way to spread the bulk of seam allowances across the quilt sandwich.

Often, more piecing of the quilt backing is fun—fun to do and also to enjoy when using the finished quilt. For quilters with a stash of fabrics, stitching many small pieces into the backing is a great way to make room for more fabric. The backing is also a place for unused quilt blocks that did not make it into the quilt top.

For hand quilters, even though pressing seams open on the quilt backing minimizes thickness, some effect on stitch size will occur. Purists will want to balance the amount of piecing of the backing with their desire to keep stitches uniformly tiny.

## Thread

Thread is a significant player in the construction of a quilt. Not only does it serve the practical purpose of holding the three layers together, but also stitching done with the thread becomes a quilt's second and equally important design element—the quilting—which is at the heart of the definition of a quilt. In a sense, this entire book is about what can be done with thread.

## Techniques

Hand quilting is done with needles labeled "betweens" or "quilting needles." These needles are very short and sturdy with round eyes. Generally, the smaller the needle, the smaller the stitches can be. Hand-quilting needles are sized in reverse: the larger the number, the smaller the needle. A size 12 quilting needle is often recommended as the ideal needle. This small needle may help achieve tiny stitches, but it also can be frustrating and time-consuming to thread. If you have trouble threading a size 12 needle, try purchasing a different brand of needles. Many brands are on the market, and they vary greatly in size of eye openings as well as thickness and sharpness of the needles themselves. Another possibility is to switch to a larger-size needle, a size 11 or size 10. Chances are, you will be able to achieve stitches just as small with these needles. The time spent attempting to thread the size 12 needle can be spent stitching a few more lines of hand quilting.

Here are some pointers to assist in needle threading:

- Wet the eye of the needle, not the thread.
- The eye of a needle is often created with a stamping process that leaves the opening on one side of the needle larger than the other. If one side seems hard to thread, try threading from the other side.
- Thread a supply of needles in the morning while your eyes are fresh.
- Have someone else thread a supply of needles for you.
- When all else fails, buy a good needle threader.

### Strength or Weight

On quilts that will be used, the general rule is that the thread should break before it cuts the fabric. If the thread is stronger than the fabric, then when the weaker element gives way—the fabric—repair will involve replacing patches in the quilt top and probably tears in the backing fabric as well. If the thread is weaker and breaks, redoing stitching is much easier.

### Hand Quilting and Thread

Unless the quilt is a wall hanging, thread for hand quilting needs to be stronger than thread for machine quilting. Hand quilting leaves behind only a single strand of thread that must bear all the stress of usage.

Cotton thread manufactured specifically for hand quilting is stronger than regular sewing thread but will not cut through cotton fabrics. It can bear the stress of the hand quilting process as well as the tugs and pulls from handling during usage.

For a wall hanging, the stress of pulling a length of thread repeatedly through the layers is still present, even though there won't be any strain from handling when the quilt is completed. Unless a specialty thread is needed for a design reason (a metallic, for example, to get sheen), using hand-quilting thread will avoid the frustration of thread breaking during stitching—or worse, thread breaking after the quilt is completed.

### Machine Quilting and Thread

Thread manufactured only for hand quilting should not be used for machine quilting. The coating on this thread will stick to the tension disks of your sewing machine.

For machine quilting, many different weights of thread can be used and still result in a quilt that will hold up well over time. This greater flexibility is possible

## Techniques

Thread is measured with a two-part numbering system. The first number indicates the size of the strand: the higher the number, the smaller the strand. The second number tells how many single strands are twisted together to make up the thread. For example, machine-embroidery thread size 60/2 designates a strand size of 60 with 2 single strands twisted to make the thread. Machine-embroidery thread also comes in size 60/3. Size 60/2 thread is finer than 60/3 because there are fewer strands twisted together. Standard sewing thread is size 50/3.

The size of the sewing machine needle must be matched to the weight of the thread to avoid skipped stitches or broken thread. Sewing machines differ. Always use the smallest needle that your machine will tolerate without skipping stitches or breaking threads. In the numbering system for sewing-machine needles, the bigger the number is, the bigger the needle will be. The following chart shows commonly used threads by weight and the accompanying needle sizes.

| Thread | Thread Size | Needle Type and Size | Bobbin Thread |
| --- | --- | --- | --- |
| Machine-embroidery thread | 60/2 | Sharp or Denim 70/10<br>Sharp 80/12<br>Quilting 75/11 | Machine-embroidery thread |
| Cotton-mercerized thread | 50/3 | Sharp or Denim 80/12<br>Quilting 75/11 | Cotton-mercerized thread |
| Cotton machine-quilting thread | 40/3 | Sharp, Denim, or Quilting 90/14 | Cotton machine-quilting thread<br>Cotton-mercerized thread<br>Machine-embroidery thread |
| Rayon thread | 40 and 30 | Embroidery 75/11<br>Sharp 90/14 | Rayon thread<br>Machine-embroidery thread |
| Invisible thread | .004 mm | Sharp or Denim 70/10<br>or 80/12<br>Quilting 75/11 | Invisible thread (wind slowly to<br>prevent thread stretching)<br>Machine-embroidery thread |
| Metallic thread | Varies | Metallic 70/10, 80/12,<br>or 90/14<br>Embroidery 90/14 | Machine-embroidery thread<br>Nylon or polyester lingerie thread,<br>also known as bobbin thread |
| Flat polyester film | n/a | Metallic 70/10<br>Sharp 80/12 or 90/14<br>Embroidery 90/14 | Nylon or polyester lingerie thread,<br>also known as bobbin thread |

because machine quilting leaves two lines of thread behind, the top and bottom threads. These two lines share the strength duty.

The weight of the thread is not the only consideration when deciding whether a particular thread is strong enough. The weight must be paired with the density of the stitching. For a bed quilt, the more space between the lines of machine quilting, the stronger the thread needs to be. A heavy thread can bear the stress of an open

## Techniques

The goal for machine stitching is not only to have stitches of even length, but also to have the tension between the top and bottom threads balanced so that a perfect stitch is formed each time. With practice, this goal can be achieved even with free-motion stitching most of the time. However, frequent changes of direction in a stitched line inevitably result in some threads pulling to the top or bottom. This problem will be much less noticeable when the color of the bobbin thread matches the color of the top thread.

quilting design. Stated in reverse, dense stitching can be done with a weaker thread because there are more threads per inch to share the load. A good general rule is to use standard sewing thread (size 50/3) or stronger for lines of stitching more than 1″ (2.5 cm) apart and for stitching used to anchor the layers together (such as stitching in-the-ditch).

Because the sewing machine places a continuous line of thread on the surface, choosing the proper weight of thread to achieve the desired design effect becomes imperative. A thick thread or a medium-weight thread quilted closely can result in a

*The Sky Is the Limit*, Heather Waldron Tewell, 48″ × 68″ (121.9 cm × 172.7 cm), machine quilted; private collection. The quilting pattern is quite dense. The majority of the machine quilting was done with machine-embroidery thread (size 60/2) to minimize the thready appearance that machine quilting can have. Because this quilt was a gift for a young person to use, the long lines of stitching and every 3″ (7.6 cm) of the background grid were done with cotton sewing thread (size 50/3) to increase the durability of the quilt.

thready appearance. When seeking to create texture and not line, use the lightest-weight thread that is strong enough for your purpose.

## Stitch Length

The goal for traditional hand quilting is small, even stitches. Until the use of big stitch and thick thread for hand quilting, showcasing the thread was not an important aspect of hand quilting. Big stitch involves stitching with thread thicker than hand-quilting thread, such as perle cotton, and using a long stitch, even as long as ¼″ (0.6 cm). While hand quilting creates texture, the longer stitch allows the thread and the dashed line to have a design impact of their own.

For machine quilters, thread is of supreme importance because of the continuous line of thread that the machine lays on the quilt surface. Machine quilters will want to play around with a longer stitch length to show the thread to advantage, especially decorative threads such as metallics and rayons. Test threads and stitch lengths on a sample. The stitched line gives the most visual pleasure when the stitch length is consistent across the quilt.

## Decorative Threads

Machine quilting has led to an explosion in the use of decorative threads. These specialty threads tend to stand out, offering a reflective quality in the stitched line that is not present with regular sewing threads. Because they are not standard in quilt making, decorative threads are generally used for nontraditional quilts.

Some kinds of thread being used are

- variegated
- metallic
- rayon
- invisible
- flat polyester film

 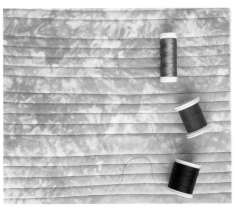

Machine sewers can achieve many different effects by their choice of thread. Rayon, metallic, polyester film, and invisible thread each will look different. Controlling the subtlety of thread can make the difference between a good quilt and a great quilt.

## Options

A few scenarios may clarify the thread selection process for machine quilting.

**Scenario 1** Susan's quilt top consists of pieced blocks alternated with plain blocks. She wants to use simple parallel lines across the pieced areas and a feathered circle filling the plain blocks. The parallel lines are a functional design intended to hold the layers together but not to be significant as lines in themselves. Using a medium-weight thread such as size 50/3 sewing thread will not give a thready appearance and will be strong enough for 1″ (2.5 cm) spacing of parallel lines. On the other hand, stitching a feathered circle puts a lot of thread in one location. Size 60/2 machine-embroidery thread will be strong enough and still avoid a thready appearance.

**Scenario 2** Mary is working on a community service quilt that she knows will be laundered frequently. She plans to stitch a 2″ (5.1 cm), diagonal grid over the entire quilt surface. Mary should use machine-quilting thread. With lines this widely spaced, even a heavy thread like machine-quilting thread will not appear thready. Using machine-quilting thread will give the quilt the durability that Mary seeks.

Variegated thread (shaded from light to dark in one color) or color-blocked thread (shaded from one color to another) will add a come-and-go effect to a line of stitching. Where the value of the thread matches the value of the patch over which it is sewn, the thread will disappear; where the thread contrasts with the patch, it will be seen. A quilting design stitched with variegated thread will alternate between creating texture and creating a visible linear design.

Rayon threads come in a wide range of variegated and solid colors. They add a subtle sheen to the surface without being shiny. Two weights are available: size 40 and 30. The size 30 thread is thicker and shinier, giving it more presence on the surface than the size 40 rayon thread.

Metallic thread has even more shine than rayon thread, with flat polyester film being the shiniest of all.

*Nababeep*, Melody Crust, 43″ × 51″ (109.2 cm × 129.5 cm), machine quilted.

Wildflowers seen on a visit to South Africa inspired this quilt. The purple and orange blooms were so bright that only flat polyester film with the most light-reflective properties could capture the intensity.

*Seattle Pet*, Heather Waldron Tewell, 15″ × 22″ (38.1 cm × 55.9 cm), hand quilted.

Metallic thread, hand stitched for the raindrops in the background and puddles in the foreground, suggests the glisten of water. The quilt is intended for the wall, so incorporating a soft thread like a metallic will not affect the longevity of the piece.

Invisible thread, either clear or smoke, takes on the color of the fabric over which it is sewn. As the ultimate disappearing thread, it leaves only texture behind. Invisible thread is a good choice when only texture is desired and the quilt top is constructed from a great variety of fabrics.

Hand sewers can experiment with threads. A thicker thread, such as perle cotton or jeans stitch, will leave a heavier line. When the stitch length is increased as well, the line and stitches become even more obvious. Hand quilting can be done with metallic thread. Because this thread is soft and tends to break easily, use shorter lengths of thread. Pieces 10″ (25.4 cm) to 12″ (30.5 cm) long will reduce breakage at the eye of the needle and along the thread's length caused by exerting more pull than the soft thread can handle. Because metallic thread does not wear well, it is best reserved for wall quilts.

## In Review

Understanding the design effects that will result from your choice of batting, backing, and thread will ensure your satisfaction in the completed quilt. The exercises that follow allow you to explore some of these choices.

1. Select five different kinds or weights of thread. On a sample quilt sandwich, using a walking foot or the even-feed feature on your sewing machine, experiment with stitch lengths. Observe the differences in the thread's sheen, visibility, and so on as the stitch length changes:

    • Stitch straight lines with an average stitch length.
    • Stitch again using a shorter stitch.
    • Stitch a third time using a much longer stitch.

2. Select five different kinds or weights of thread. On a sample quilt sandwich, hand stitch a short line with each thread. Observe the differences in each thread's sheen, visibility, and so on.

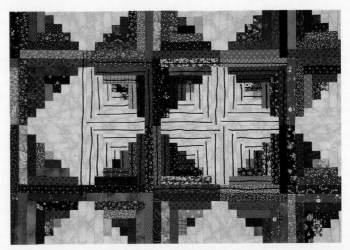

A Log Cabin quilt top is a traditional pattern. If the goal is to create an authentic old feeling for the completed quilt, a bit of research will lead to the kinds of designs pioneer stitchers used. If traditional style is not important here, the choices for quilting designs are unlimited.

The nature of the Log Cabin block creates two easily identifiable plans for the quilting design. One plan repeats the square blocks used in the quilt's construction. The second plan ignores the block construction and emphasizes the dark and light areas formed where four blocks join.

A third alternative is an overall stitching design. For hand quilters, this possibility is not attractive due to the overwhelming number of seams that must be crossed. Machine quilters can consider this option. Thread color will be an issue, however. A value of thread that matches the dark areas will show when crossing the light areas, and a light value of thread matching the light areas will show when crossing the dark areas. The benefit of an overall design—its continuous stitching—will be lost if the thread must be changed every time it crosses a patch of a different value. One solution is to choose a medium value of thread that will show equally crossing the dark and light patches. Because the thread will show, the lines themselves will become an element of the design, in addition to the texture created by the stitching. Another solution is to use invisible thread.

The simplest of all designs for the Log Cabin block is to stitch down the center of each log. A hand quilter will find these short lines easier to do than will a machine quilter because of the numerous starts and stops. No marking is required. Light thread can easily be used on the light areas and medium-dark thread on the dark ones. Such a simple design works well when the quilt top is already visually complex due to the variety of fabrics, value contrast, and numerous patches.

For any of the sketched designs requiring stitching down the center of each log, the batting options will be much greater than for the more open shape-and-background-filler designs suggested. With ¾" (1.9 cm) logs, the stitching lines will be ¾" (1.9 cm) apart, making a fairly dense quilting pattern. This density of stitching will meet the manufacturer's requirement for nearly all battings except perhaps a 100 percent cotton batting. The shape-and-background-filler sketches have areas that are more open, necessitating a batting whose fibers will not migrate when lines of stitching are more widely spaced, such as polyester battings, cotton/polyester-blend battings, or needle-punched, 100 percent cotton battings.

*(continues)*

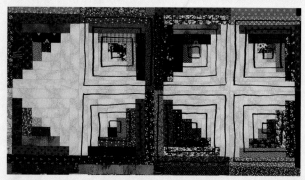

A slight variation on stitching down the center of each log is to form concentric squares. Assuming the quilting will be accomplished by hand, the same medium-value thread might be chosen for all the stitching. The greater contrast between thread and fabric in some areas than others will barely be noticeable. This design has one drawback not present on the previous sketch: the lines cross over seam allowances. A two-block stitched sample will help you determine whether the effect of the concentric-square design is worth the extra effort of crossing seam allowances.

Machine stitchers who want to practice their free-motion technique may consider reversing the placement of the feathers and grid. Lack of precision in stitching the feathered wreath will not show nearly as much against the medium-dark fabrics as against the light-colored ones. The effect of the curves on the surface will be lessened, but perhaps the gain in free-motion confidence is worth this small sacrifice.

The grid sketched is an even one created by a line down the center of every other log. Stitching this more open pattern will mean the batting must allow for lines at least 1½" (3.8 cm) apart (the distance between the midpoints of two logs).

Machine quilters can use designs on a Log Cabin quilt that a hand quilter would never attempt because of the numerous seams. Knowing that quilting shows best on light-colored fabrics, a feathered wreath, redesigned for continuous free-motion stitching, can fill the light area. Choosing this traditional motif will help maintain the old feeling of the quilt.

Straight lines of background filler can be stitched across the dark areas. Although these lines could be evenly spaced, the lines sketched are parallel but not evenly spaced to give a nontraditional feeling.

Some filler lines are necessary across the center of the wreath to maintain the even density. These lines can be on the diagonal, as shown, but they can also be parallel to the background grid. Small changes sometimes make an enormous difference.

This sketch is an example of shapes positioned side by side to create the design. To enhance the uniform density, the floral shapes are positioned so that a leaf points to the V in its neighbor and not to another point. The design could be easily machine stitched using tear-away paper. Minimal straight filler lines are suggested. More lines may need to be introduced during the stitching process to keep the spacing relatively even.

The backing fabric must be chosen here with particular attention to its value. Dark fabrics on the back will shadow through the light fabrics on the top.

*Blue Jeans*, Melody Crust and Heather Waldron Tewell, 50″ × 61″ (127 cm × 154.9 cm), machine quilted.

The finished quilt uses the design seen in the top right sketch on page 112. By a quilter with good technical skills, a free-motion design like this can be stitched successfully over even the lightest areas where quilting shows the most. Straight lines over the darker patches complement the curves. In spite of this quilt's relatively small size, the quilting took more than three spools of thread. One spool of navy blue thread was used for the straight lines in the dark areas. Regular-weight sewing thread (size 50/3) was chosen because these lines are spaced greater than 1″ (2.5 cm) apart. For the feathered wreaths where the lines of stitching are closer together, two spools of light blue machine-embroidery thread (size 60/2) were used.

# CHAPTER SEVEN

# Marking and Basting

*B*ATTING, BACKING, AND THREAD as well as fabrics in the quilt top are materials sewn into a quilt during the quilting process. Each must be carefully selected for quality and impact on the design for a quilter's vision to be achieved. Marking and basting are processes that support the realization of a well-designed and well-constructed quilt. When properly done, marking and basting leave no traces in the finished quilt.

A water buffalo grazes on terraced rice fields near Yuanjiang, Yunnan Province, China. The Chinese rice farmer divides his terraced fields into units to control the water. Without careful preparation, farming on these steep slopes would be impossible. Although the quilter's task is not as arduous, careful attention to the basting step is necessary and will make the quilting process go more smoothly. Terraced fields in China, medieval stone walls in Yorkshire, or fenced ranches in Texas—all are great inspirations for the quilting design.

Marking is especially subject to problems. Many tools leave a visible line that is easily followed during quilting. While this is an asset, the marks these tools make are not necessarily easy to remove or may be set permanently by heat, including by simply leaving the quilt in a sun-filled room. The best practice is to use tools producing marks that can be removed reliably, limit marking as much as possible, or use one of the many suggested procedures for which no marking is needed.

Proper basting is equally as important as careful marking. The entire quilting process will be much more enjoyable and can be accomplished smoothly when the layers are securely aligned and the puff of the batting is under control with good basting technique.

## Marking

A quilter usually needs some lines to follow when stitching through the layers. To preserve the beauty of the finished quilt, these lines should become invisible either after the stitching is done or once the quilt is washed. Several tools are available to accomplish this purpose, and several different methods may be employed. In some cases, a line to follow can be created without leaving a mark on the quilt's surface at all.

Ideally, a marking tool makes a dark enough line on the quilt top so it can be seen for stitching yet leaves no trace once the quilting is completed. Two of the best tools are the silver marking pencil and the white chalk pencil.

### Silver Marking Pencil

The silver marking pencil is a wonderful tool. It sharpens to a fine point. If its point is kept sharp the line stays thin, ensuring that it can be removed easily or will simply wear away as the stitching is accomplished. Using gentle pressure to make the mark avoids leaving a wider and darker line than necessary.

A mark created by the silver pencil is visible on most colors of fabric, but it can be hard to see on grays and other grayed fabrics in the same value range. A white chalk pencil is an alternative tool to use on these fabrics.

The downside of the silver marking pencil is its tendency to wear away before all lines are stitched. To avoid this problem, do not mark the entire quilt top before stitching. Plan the entire design, but mark only an area approximately 12″ (30.5 cm) square immediately before stitching.

### White Chalk Pencil

The white chalk pencil is a good substitute when the silver pencil line cannot be seen. A chalk line, however, tends to rub away even faster than a silver line. Be careful when handling a quilt that has been marked with chalk to preserve the lines as long as they are needed. As with the silver pencil, be sure to keep the point sharp for a finer line, and do not mark too large an area.

Chalk comes in colors other than white. Unfortunately, although lines made with these colors may be more visible, the dyes used in colored chalks can sometimes be difficult to remove.

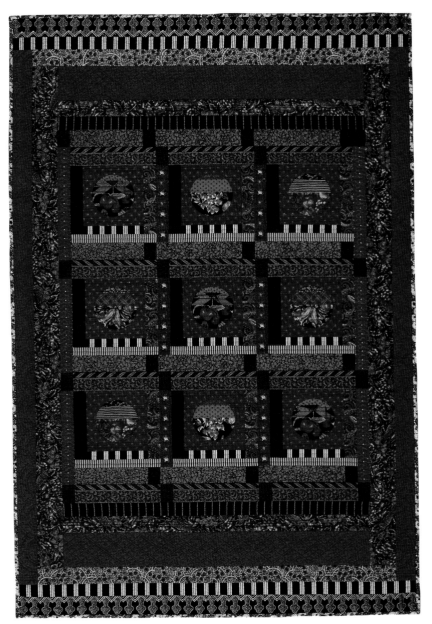

*Magic Carpet of Falling Fruits and Vegetables*, Heather Waldron Tewell, 46″ × 73″
(116.8 cm × 185.4 cm), hand quilted.

The quilting for the "fringe" on this "carpet" was done by simply outlining the design in
the fabric. No marking was necessary. The rest of the quilting was marked with either a
silver or white chalk marking pencil.

## Other Tools

An abundance of other tools for marking is available, with more being added all the
time. If you want to explore these options, test them first on every fabric in the quilt.
Read the manufacturer's instructions on how to remove the line, and follow them
exactly. Be sure that you can get the result you want following the manufacturer's
instructions before using the tool on your quilt.

A light table can be improvised
by spreading the dining room
table as if to put in additional
leaves but instead placing a
sheet of Plexiglas (perhaps from
an old picture frame) across the
opening. Then place a table
lamp on the floor under the
glass. If necessary, remove the
lamp shade for a stronger light.

# Ways to Approach Marking

Marking can be divided into two basic methods: design under and design over. The method that works for a particular quilt depends upon the kind of quilting design chosen and the opaqueness of the fabrics in the quilt top.

## *Design-Under Method*

The design-under method can only be done before the quilt is basted. Because the design must be seen through the quilt top, the fabrics in the top need to be of a medium to light value. Sometimes, you can see the design more easily through the top by working on a light table. Black, navy blue, and similar dark fabrics are too opaque to be used with this method.

To use the design-under method, follow these steps:

1. Draw the quilting design on freezer paper or white butcher paper using a black felt-tip marker with permanent ink. A heavy mark makes the design easy to see through the fabric.
2. Tape the design to a table.
3. Lay the quilt top over the design, moving the top until the design is perfectly positioned.
4. Weight the top down with books or other easy-to-handle items placed away from the design area. The weights keep the top from shifting position.
5. Trace the design onto the quilt top using either a silver pencil or white chalk pencil.

The design-under method is most successful on small to medium-size pieces. All of the marking can be done in advance without fear that the lines will rub away before they can be stitched. If some lines do become faint, lightly going over them just before stitching will make them visible again. On large quilts the silver or chalk pencil lines will likely disappear due to the amount of handling necessary to complete the stitching.

## *Design-Over Method*

Design-over methods can be done either before or after the quilt is sandwiched. They involve creating a pattern that can be outlined onto the quilt top. Plastic templates, also called stencils, are widely available and come in a great variety of sizes and styles. When the selection does not include one that is the right size, make your own. Learning to make templates is not difficult and ensures that your design suits a space exactly.

Although marking on a quilt top before it is basted is a little easier to do—the fabric ripples less as lines are drawn—marking an entire quilt top before quilting is very time-consuming, and lines made with the silver or chalk pencils may wear away before they are stitched.

To ensure that the marked lines will be visible when you need them, use one of two procedures or a combination of both:

1. Plan the entire design, cut your stencils or templates to fit, but do not mark on the quilt top before basting. If necessary, make simple registration marks with

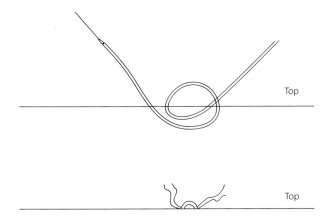

*Spring Churn Dash.*

When the placement of a quilting stencil has been figured out, all of the marking need not be done before basting. Use tailor tacks or pins to mark where the stencil fits; then baste. When you reach the area covered by the stencil, line the stencil up with the registration marks and, using a silver or chalk pencil, mark the design; then quilt it. See full quilt on page 69.

To make a tailor tack, complete the following steps:

1. Thread a needle with regular sewing thread, matching the lengths of the tails.
2. Take a ⅛″ (0.3 cm) stitch in the fabric.
3. Pull the thread until about 1″ (2.5 cm) of both tails extends above the surface.
4. Take another stitch in nearly the same place.
5. Pull the thread until a stitch forms on the surface.
6. Cut the thread, leaving 1″ (2.5 cm) tails in both threads.

tailor tacks or safety pins so that the template can be repositioned precisely. After basting, use your precut patterns to mark only the area that you can quilt within the hoop or immediately ahead of your needle.

2. Plan the design. Mark the major lines before basting. After basting, machine quilters can stitch the drawn lines first before the marks have a chance to disappear. Then fill in between the major lines, marking as needed from the top. For example, if a ¾″ (1.9 cm) grid is planned, mark every third line before basting. The two lines in between can be marked from the top after basting or can be stitched using a sewing guide on the machine. Because the process of hand quilting is usually done from the center working out, hand quilters may find that some lines have become faint by the time they get to that area. A little re-marking will make them visible again.

## Techniques for Not Marking

Several materials and techniques make it possible not to place a single mark on the quilt. These may not work on every quilt, but knowing about them may give you more options as you plan the quilting design.

### Tear-Away Paper

Machine quilters have another design-over method available to them: tear-away paper. Tear-away paper, also known as "doctor's examination room paper," is available in most quilt stores and catalogs. Simply draw the design onto the surface of the paper, pin or tape it to the quilt that has been sandwiched, and stitch through. When the entire design has been stitched, tear away the paper. To make identical copies of the same design, follow these steps:

1. Unthread your sewing machine, top and bobbin.
2. Insert a large-size, old needle such as a Sharp 90/14.
3. Draw the design on one piece of tear-away paper using a felt-tip pen with permanent ink. Pencil is not recommended because it will transfer to the thread when stitched.
4. Staple or pin several layers of the tear-away paper under the sheet with the drawn design. Place the staples or pins away from the drawn lines.
5. Stitch through all layers at the same time, using a short stitch length.

The large needle and short stitch combine to make the design both easy to see and easy to tear away.

## Interfacing

In some cases, interfacing can be used instead of template plastic or cardboard. To use this method, complete the following steps:

1. Draw the shape to be quilted onto a piece of stiff interfacing using a permanent pen.
2. Cut out the design.
3. Pin or thread baste the pattern onto the quilt.
4. Stitch around the pattern about ⅛″ (0.3 cm) from the outer edge.
5. Remove the interfacing pattern.

Interfacing is a viable alternative to a stencil when the design is an outlined shape. Details, if any, inside the outlined shape can be drawn or stitched freehand after the interfacing is removed. Lines from the outer edge of the design continuing into the center cannot be stitched through interfacing because interfacing will not tear away. For these kinds of designs, a template is necessary.

For hand quilters, interfacing works well because it is a pliable material and will bend along with the fabric as the quilting stitches are formed.

*Sherbet.*

Designs that can be outlined lend themselves to templates made from interfacing. The small details inside the shape can be added later. See full quilt on page 74.

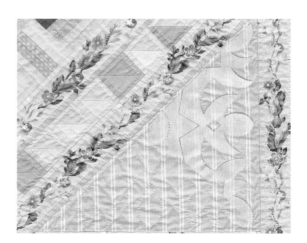

## Design in Fabric

Some fabrics have designs that can be stitched. These fabrics can be used on either the front or the back of the quilt. If used on the front of the quilt, the fabric will, of course, need to work with the other elements of the quilt top's design. Sometimes, serendipity steps in, and a fabric in the quilt top just -happens to provide lines for a good stitching pattern.

Look for regularly repeating geometrics, florals with well-defined motifs, and representational prints on which the design elements are well spaced.

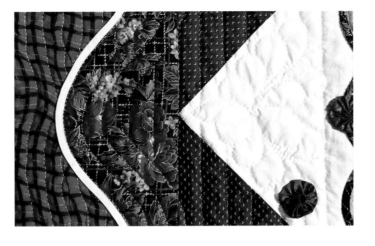

*Six Blonde Ladies.* The quilting was drawn with a variety of methods. The stitching in the outer border follows a line in the undulating striped fabric, requiring no marking. The feathers were marked with a silver pencil following a stencil, the parallel straight lines with a chalk pencil and ruler. See full quilt on page 4.

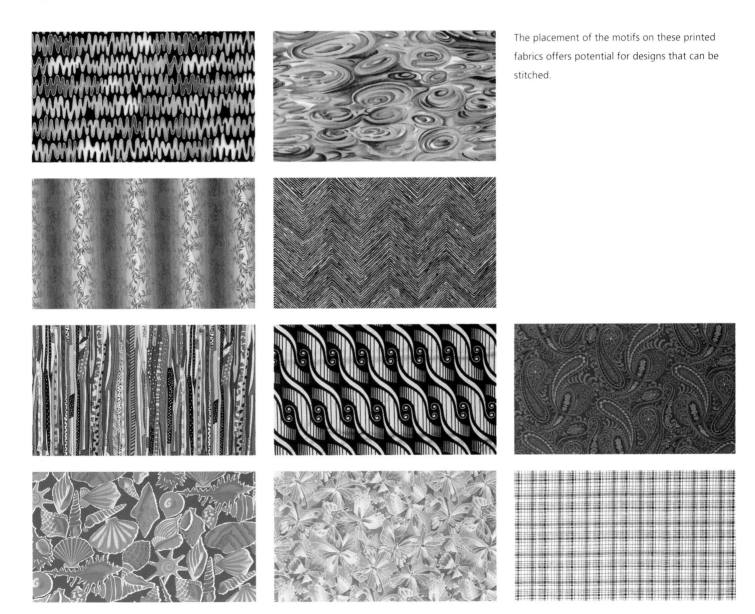

The placement of the motifs on these printed fabrics offers potential for designs that can be stitched.

In some cases, the stitching design will need to be worked out in advance. Using a pencil and a scrap of the fabric (or a photocopy), draw samples of your stitching ideas until you have the right one for the quilt. Remember that the amount of the quilting needs to be adequate for the batting you have chosen and that the lines should be evenly distributed.

When the fabric with an appropriate stitching design is planned for the backing, be careful to match the print across any seams necessary to make the backing large enough. Taking this step will maintain the regularity of the stitching design on the front. In addition to an overall pattern, a design of shapes and background filler can be created by machine stitching on the backing with this method:

1. Mark the quilting design for the shapes on the front of the quilt and stitch them first from the front.
2. Turn the quilt over. The bobbin thread will become the thread on the front of the quilt; the thread in the sewing machine needle will be on the back.
3. Stitch with the back of the quilt facing up, following the design in the backing fabric and avoiding the shapes stitched from the front.

## Free-Motion Stitching

Machine quilters also have the technique of free-motion stitching available to them as a no-marking option. The stitching design can be worked out with pencil and paper before it is sewn. Actually, drawing the design with pencil and paper is a good warm-up exercise. Some skill is needed to fill the spaces uniformly and to anticipate where the design should go next.

Free-motion stitching can be used as an overall design for the quilt top, or it can be a background filler pattern combined with shapes.

## Eyeballing

No marking is necessary if the eye has a line to follow. In echo quilting, the eye follows the edge of the patch. Each successive line can simply be eyeballed as the concentric rings get larger. For machine quilters, the edge of the darning foot can be used as a guide to enhance accuracy and avoid marking.

In outline quilting, a line of stitching is placed about ¼″ (0.6 cm) away from the seam. For hand quilters, this placement avoids stitching through the layers of the seam allowance. Eyeballing an even distance from the seam can be done easily. When outlining by machine, quilters can use the edge of the presser foot as a guide.

Playing around with lines across fabrics with potential for stitching designs can lead to interesting possibilities for the quilting.

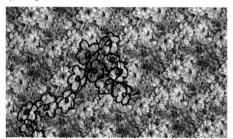
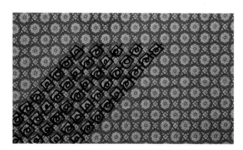

Some lines of stitching are short enough that they can be accurately stitched without drawing. A quilted X through a 2″ (5.1 cm) or 3″ (7.6 cm) square can be eye-balled. When the pieced design is a nine-patch, the entire quilting design can be eye-balled if it consists of an X through each square. While this may be easy to do, take care that the quilting design also complements the quilt top.

## Presser Foot and Sewing Guide

Machine quilters can use the edge of the presser foot and the sewing-guide attachment to create equidistant lines. A preexisting line must be present on the quilt top as an aid in stitching the first line. This line can be a seam or series of seams or it can be marked with one of the pencils ahead of time. For example, to create a 1″ (2.5 cm) design of evenly spaced parallel lines, complete the following steps:

1. Before the top is basted, draw parallel lines every 4″ (10.2 cm) using the silver marking pencil.
2. Baste the quilt.
3. Using the walking or even-feed feature, stitch on the 4″ (10.2 cm) lines.
4. Attach the sewing guide to your machine and set it to stitch 2″ (5.1 cm) from the line.
5. Stitch 2″ (5.1 cm) lines between all 4″ (10.2 cm) lines.
6. Reset the sewing guide to stitch 1″ (2.5 cm) from the line.
7. Stitch all 1″ (2.5 cm) lines.

By starting large and halving the space between the lines each time, you substantially reduce the possibility of sewing puckers into the quilt's surface.

## Scratching a Line

For short distances, a line can be made on the quilt's surface by scratching with a tool. Early quilters used their hand-quilting needle to make an indentation that they could follow. More recent quilters use an old sewing-machine needle because the shank is larger to grasp. The *hera* marker is a tool made especially for the purpose of scratching a line.

The trick of scratching a line is worth remembering. It will not work for marking too far in advance of stitching or for very large areas, but it can be ideal over short distances. Scratched lines leave no traces of themselves.

# Basting

The purpose of basting is to hold the three layers of a quilt together temporarily. Basting maintains the relationship of the quilt top to the quilt back while the quilting is done. It makes the process of quilting, by hand or machine, easier by reducing the need to fight the fluff of the batting. Good basting ensures that the finished quilt will be flat and square without puckers.

The importance of good basting technique cannot be overemphasized.

Stitching parallel lines in the same direction will reduce rippling between the lines. Choose one line as the centerline. Stitch all lines on one side of the centerline in the same direction. Turn the bulk of the quilt. Stitch the remaining lines in the opposite direction. When you use this method, only two lines side by side will be stitched in opposite directions.

Two other methods are being employed by today's quilters:

1. The basting gun inserts a plastic clip through the layers. The clip can be inserted from top to back, or it can be done like a stitch, going through the top, out the back, and returning to the top. Some people find that the clips do not hold the layers in place adequately; others love the tool.

2. The second method is a basting spray, much like spray adhesive for photographs. The wrong side of the backing fabric is sprayed with the basting spray and then hand pressed flat against the batting. The backing is then sprayed and hand pressed to the other side of the batting. For small pieces, the basting spray will hold the layers long enough to quilt. For large pieces, however, the spray can release before the job is done.

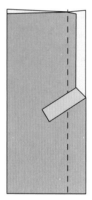

To grade a seam, trim away ⅛" (0.3 cm) of the darker fabric along the seam allowance.

## Techniques

Liquid spray starch that comes in a pump sprayer does not flake like starch in an aerosol can. If you're using starch in an aerosol can, let it sink into the fabric before ironing. Concentrated starch in a ratio of half water to half starch works well.

## *Basic Methods*

Two methods can be used: thread basting and pin basting. Thread basting is usually done on quilts that will be hand quilted. Pins tend to get in the way of the quilting hoop, and thread will catch on them during the quilting process. On quilts to be machine stitched, pin basting is the usual method. The basting process goes faster, and pins can be removed from in front of the sewing machine needle as the quilting is being done. Threads from basting also tend to be difficult to remove following machine quilting. However, mavericks exist who choose to pin baste a hand-quilted piece or thread baste a machine-quilted one. Whichever method is used, the process must be done properly to ensure the success of the finished quilt.

## *Preparation of Top and Backing*

Before beginning to sandwich the layers, press the quilt top and backing. Ironing with spray starch can make the quilt slip along the bed of the sewing machine smoothly.

To spread the thickness of the seam allowances in both the quilt top and backing, press open as many seam allowances as possible. Where opening the seam allowance is not possible due to the quilt-block construction, be sure that the seam allowances are pressed to the same side down the entire length of the seam. Remove any loose, dark threads that may show behind light fabrics. If seams with dark fabrics are pressed to the light fabric side, grade the seams as necessary.

## *Basting on a Table*

Both thread and pin basting can be done either on the floor or on a table. Basting on a table is less stressful on the knees and back. A 3′ × 6′ (91 cm × 183 cm) craft table is ideal. Most quilt shops are happy to allow you to baste in an empty classroom. Public libraries and community centers often have tables available, too. Sitting in a chair with wheels speeds the process along. If no table is available or the table process seems cumbersome, laying the quilt flat on a carpet, wood, or linoleum floor is an acceptable alternative.

Lay the backing fabric right side down, and center it on the table. Use binder clips to hold the fabric taut wherever it drapes over the side of the table, and use masking tape where the edge of the backing fabric rests on the tabletop.

Center the batting on the table, using your hands to smooth out any ripples.

Center the quilt top over the batting and backing. Use a ruler, or anything with a square corner, to adjust the quilt top so that the corners are square and the lines of piecing are straight. Smooth in place and baste.

To baste on a table, complete these ten steps:

1. Tape a toothpick to the table at the centers of all four sides, at 90 degrees to the table edges. These markers will allow you to feel the table centers through the backing and additional layers as they are added.

2. Center the backing fabric right side down on the table, making sure that the centers on all sides of the table line up with the centers of the backing.

3. Fasten the backing fabric securely to the table. Use binder clips (also called bulldog clips, available at office supply stores) where the fabric drapes over the table, placing four to five per side. Use masking tape where a raw edge of the fabric rests on the table. For very large quilts, all four sides will drape and need to be fastened with binder clips. Use a pot holder to open the clips if they hurt your hands. The backing should be taut but not distorted or stretched.

4. Lay the batting on top of the backing, matching centers. Gently smooth out any wrinkles without distorting the batting. Do not fasten it to the table.

5. Center the quilt top, right side up, on the table with the backing and batting. Do not fasten it to the table. With your hands, smooth out any wrinkles or puckers. Carefully check to see that no distortion has occurred in the pieced or appliquéd designs. All right angles should be square and all straight lines straight. Use a straight or square ruler, as necessary, to check. Adjust the quilt top until the alignment is perfect.

6. Starting in the center, place 1″ (2.5 cm) safety pins (size 1) approximately 4″ (10.2 cm) apart in staggered rows about 3″ (7.6 cm) apart across the entire quilt draped over the tabletop. (At this point, the layers could be thread basted starting from the center.) Most people's knuckles measure approximately 4″ (10.2 cm) across and can be used as a convenient measuring device. Where possible, insert pins out of the way of anticipated lines of quilting. Place pins in the same direction to make removal easier. Do not close pins yet.

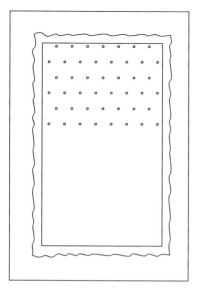

Pins should be placed in offset rows about every 3″ (7.6 cm).

7. Remove the binder clips and masking tape. Slide the pinned portion of the sandwich to one side of the table until it nearly falls off the table's edge. Repeat the process of smoothing the back and anchoring the loose edges with clips or tape. The weight of the quilt is enough to anchor the fourth side; do not clip. Spread the batting and quilt top across the backing. Center the sides of the backing on the side centers of the top. Check to be sure that the design lines of the quilt top remain straight and square; adjust as necessary. Pin.

8. Continue to work, repositioning the layers across the table until the entire quilt has been pinned.

9. Turn the quilt over, checking for puckers or excess fabric.

10. Close all pins.

## Basting on the Floor

Floor basting allows you to secure all four sides of the backing fabric before layering on the batting and quilt top.

To thread baste on the floor, follow these steps:

1. Lay the backing right side down on the floor. If the floor is a hard surface like linoleum or wood, use masking tape to secure the backing to the floor. Painter's masking tape (often blue) leaves no residue behind, making it a better choice than regular masking tape. If the floor is carpeted, use T-pins; they push more easily than regular sewing pins and do not bend as readily. (Note: Thread basting on a looped pile carpet is not recommended. The basting threads will catch in the loops.)

2. Spread the quilt batting over the backing, matching the center of the batting to the center of the backing. Gently smooth out any wrinkles without distorting the batting.

3. Center the quilt top on the batting and backing. Smooth out any ripples, and make sure straight lines are straight and square corners are at right angles. (At this point, the layers can be pin basted starting from the center.)

4. Using an embroidery or other large-eyed needle and regular sewing thread, baste the layers together starting in the middle of the quilt and working to the edge. A 3″ (7.6 cm) grid of basting is sufficient to hold the layers together for quilting.

## Techniques

When taping to the floor, think in opposites. The first piece of tape goes in the middle of the top of the backing fabric. The second piece goes in the middle of the opposite side. The third piece goes in the middle of one of the remaining sides. The fourth piece goes in the middle of the last side. For all except the first piece of tape, apply the tape first to the fabric. The tape can then be used for pulling gently before pressing it to the floor. The diagram shows the order for securing the rest of the edges. When taping is completed, the backing fabric should be taut without ripples.

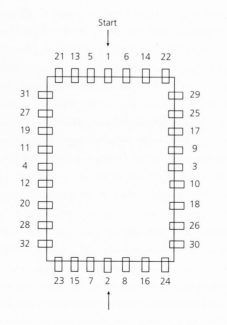

## Techniques

Thread baste starting in the vertical or horizontal center of the sandwich and basting to the edge each time. Begin again in the center and baste to the opposite edge. Start in the center a third time and baste to one of the other sides. Last, start in the center and baste to the remaining edge. Four knots will be in the center of the quilt, and the lines of basting will form a plus sign through the quilt.

Baste the entire quilt in a 12″ (30.5 cm) grid. Starting about 12″ (30.5 cm) from the center knot and on the horizontal axis, baste to the top edge. Start in the same place and baste to the bottom edge. Start 12″ (30.5 cm) in the opposite direction from the center and baste to the top. Start in the same place and baste to the bottom.

Next do the horizontal lines on either side of the central horizontal line, each time starting in the center and working out to the edge. Complete the 12″ (30.5 cm) grid by alternating vertical and horizontal lines.

When the 12″ (30.5 cm) grid is completed, the basting can be finished in place, or the sandwich can be lifted onto a table and stitched down to a 3″ (7.6 cm) grid using the same order.

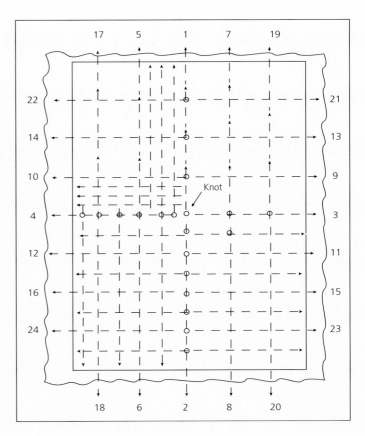

Avoid using dark threads on a light quilt top for basting. Sometimes, excess dye will rub off on the quilt top during the basting process. A soup spoon held in the opposite hand from the needle can be used as a lever to catch the tip of the needle, which tends to get buried in the quilt batting. For those quilters who find kneeling on the floor to be strenuous, a helpful procedure is to first thread baste a 12″ (30.5 cm) grid on the floor. Then pick up the quilt, lay it on a large table, and complete the basting process.

## Securing the Edges

Whether basting has been done with pins or thread, the outer edge will have batting exposed. As a last step, fold excess backing over the batting and secure it to the edge of the quilt top with thread basting or pins. Encasing the batting prevents it from shredding during the quilting process and keeps fibers from being transferred to the quilt surface.

The sandwich is ready for stitching through the layers using the quilting design you have created.

To safeguard the raw edges of the quilt top and prevent the batting from tearing during the quilting process, bring the backing over the batting, overlap the quilt top by about ½″ (1.3 cm), and baste all the way around.

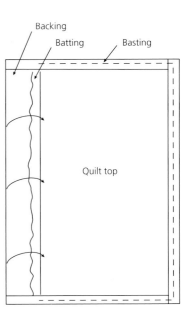

For the Mariner's Compass blocks, the seams in the piecing can serve as guides for the quilting design. Only minimal marking may be necessary in these areas.

A Mariner's Compass block has many seams and tiny points. To avoid hand stitching through seams, quilting lines can be stitched up the middle or around the inside of the larger patches.

For both hand and machine quilters, either pink or white thread can be used across the Mariner's Compass blocks without making a thready appearance (unless, of course, a very thick thread is used in machine stitching). The pink fabrics are of a medium to light value, and the patches are not large. Without significant contrast in either color or value, the visibility of the thread itself is low.

This traditional quilt top is very simple: little contrast in color, little piecing compared with the amount of white space, and a predictable layout of blocks. A plain top like this is ideal for intricate quilting designs.

Marking the quilting for a nearly all-white quilt top can be challenging. If you're stitching by machine, one option for transferring the quilting designs onto the open white areas is to stitch the designs through tear-away paper. This method will work well for shapes. For hand quilting and for other kinds of designs stitched by machine, the silver marking pencil is the best choice. Taking care to keep the pencil sharp and to mark with a light touch will ensure that the lines are no darker than necessary.

Because the fabrics in this top are very light, the design-under and the design-over methods will work equally well. If a feathered design is preferred, the design-under method is the best choice. Drawing feathers onto a piece of paper for tracing through fabric is easier than cutting a stencil. Because the silver pencil marks can wear away during the quilting process, especially the longer process of hand quilting, some re-marking may be necessary.

This design for hand stitching involves crossing over more seam allowances than the previous one. Although the design appears to give more emphasis to the compass points, the actual effect in stitching will probably be less. The X in the center circle can be stitched as a plus sign instead, to line up with the straight lines suggested for the vertical and horizontal compass points. A subtle adjustment can sometimes make a design sing.

A machine stitcher may emphasize the circular nature of the compass block, taking advantage of the compass's shape and the machine's ease with long lines of stitching. The zigzag repeats the points in the block. While this sketch shows some filler lines in the center of the block, more filler will be needed between the inner ring of twin zigzags and the outer ring to maintain an even density. Perhaps simply repeating one more ring of the zigzag will accomplish the purpose.

This block and set are in the traditional style and call for the use of traditional motifs. The spaces between the Mariner's Compass blocks are ideal for the placement of a fancy shape like the traditional feathered wreath. Care must be taken so that the size of the wreath complements the size of the compass circles. This design is too small and tight.

Because the background fabric is white, the batting must also be white. An off-white batting will change the crispness of the white fabric. Many cotton and cotton/polyester blends come in pure white. The batting choice will also be affected by how dense the quilting design is.

Another idea for machine quilting uses a free-motion stitched spiral in the center of the compass, combined with outlining of the compass points. This sketch enhances the starlike nature of the compass block in a way that the previous sketches do not.

(continues)

After the previous design was enlarged on a photocopier a few times and the different sizes tried out, this feathered wreath was found to fit the space nicely. Some background filler lines, such as the straight lines sketched, will make the wreath stand out and maintain the even density of the quilting.

The inner sawtooth border and outer white border can be treated either as two distinct areas or as one. The design sketched for the sawtooth border can be stitched without marking; the seams in the piecing are available as a guide. The parallel lines suggested for the background of the feathered wreaths can be repeated in the white border for a simple treatment. The scallop serves as a divider between the parallel lines in the white border and the grid over the sawtooth triangles. With the divider, the parallel lines will not have to line up perfectly.

Changing the direction of the parallel lines at the midpoints on each side will add a little interest as well as avoid a potential problem. When all diagonal lines are stitched in the same direction, the quilt can be pulled out of square.

The parallel lines will be most accurate if marked with the silver pencil before the quilt is sandwiched. The puffiness added by the batting can make drawing accurate lines difficult after the quilt is basted. Although it may be necessary to trace over lines later, the extra effort is preferable to inaccurate marking.

To add an opulent look and increase the complexity of the design on this otherwise rather simple top, the outer white border can be stitched by hand or machine with an undulating feathered wave. This stitching will take considerably more time than a quilted border of simple parallel lines, so the answer to the preliminary question, How much time is there for this project? must have been "Plenty."

This quilt has a formal feeling, so the vertical and horizontal waves of feathers need to resolve at the corners gracefully and not simply run off the ends or butt into each other. This sketch shows one wave ending in an elegant plume and the other simply growing out of it.

The sawtooth border is not given its own design in this sketch. It is unified with the background of the compass blocks and the feathered wave by having the same parallel lines.

*Peppermint*, Melody Crust and Heather Waldron Tewell, 63″ × 76″ (160 cm × 193 cm), machine quilted.

The quilting design uses a feathered wreath and a feathered vine combined with a background grid. Feathers used in the large plain areas complement this traditional Mariner's Compass design. The simple solution of creating mirror-image designs with one wave dying into the other allows the corner resolution to appear formal even though the wave is not continuous.

The feathered circles, feathered waves, and every other line of the background grid were marked using a silver marking pencil and the design-under method. Notice that the background grid is on the vertical and horizontal grain in the center of the quilt. This direction was chosen to allow for the longest lines of continuous machine stitching. The grid in the border is on the diagonal for extra interest.

The compass blocks themselves were quilted very simply with concentric circles. Stitching a circle inside the appliquéd circle at the center of each compass proved to be too difficult to do accurately. The principle of repetition was applied to come up with a grid design instead.

# Bindings, Labels, and Sleeves

When the quilting design has been stitched through the layers, the quilt is nearly complete. For some quilters, the last step is to bind the raw edges. Other quilters look beyond the binding. They have a personal rule that a quilt is not finished until the maker's name is on it and a sleeve for hanging has been sewn to the back. Quilters who enjoy entering competitions or who want to maintain an accurate inventory of their work include getting the quilt photographed in their list of final steps.

Azaleas in bloom, Washington Park Arboretum, Seattle, Washington. Against this exuberance of bloom, the sign tells what the arboretum visitor may not know: these are azaleas. On a quilt the label provides the essential information of quilt maker, date, and place. Patterns in tree bark and trees in bloom are among the many sources of inspiration you may find in photographs of nature.

By your having a mind-set to include not only binding but also label, sleeve, and photograph as part of the finishing, your quilts will always be ready for showing without last-minute preparation. They will never leave the house without proper identification. Also, when your quilt is unfolded many years from now, the maker's name will be known and not anonymous, the unfortunate fate of the makers of so many beautiful quilts from pioneer days.

# Bindings

Choosing the binding's fabric and style presents one last opportunity to sew your creative spirit into the finished quilt. Think about its selection carefully. The binding, sensitively done, will enhance the overall appearance of the quilt.

## Trimming the Quilt

The process of hand or machine quilting often pulls a quilt slightly out of square. Trimming the quilt before applying the binding ensures that the finished quilt will be square and the outer edges straight.

To trim a quilt, complete the following steps:

- Using a large square ruler, trim one corner first, allowing for the finished width of the binding beyond the seam line. For example, if the finished width of the binding is to be ⅜″ (0.95 cm), make the cut ⅜″ (0.95 cm) beyond where the seam will be.
- Switch to a long ruler such as a 24″ (61 cm) see-through ruler and extend the cut edge toward the next corner.
- As the corner approaches, return to the square ruler, and cut the corner.
- Repeat these steps until all four corners are cut.
- Check for accuracy by laying the quilt flat on a table or a clean floor.
- Bring the top and bottom edges to the middle. All edges should meet precisely. If they do not, mark the excess with straight pins, return the quilt to the cutting table, and recut as necessary.
- Repeat this process by bringing the left and right sides to the middle. Mark the excess, if any, and retrim as needed.

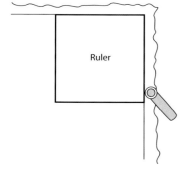

To trim the edge of the quilt before applying the binding, lay a square ruler at the corner, using the marks on the ruler to position the corner precisely. Cut both edges.

### Techniques

For those wary of cutting, a more labor-intensive but perhaps more comfortable method is possible. Instead of cutting right away, use a pencil to make a line ½″ (1.3 cm) plus the width of the binding wider than the projected cutting line (this mark will be made on the batting, not on the quilt top). If the marked line becomes crooked or a mistake is made, no harm is done. Simply revise the line until it is right, then cut ½″ (1.3 cm) inside the line.

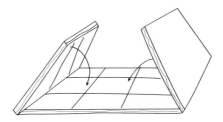
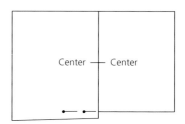

When all four sides of a quilt have been trimmed, check for accuracy. Lay the quilt on a flat surface. Bring the top and bottom to the middle, matching the centers of each end. If one edge is wider than the other, place pins as the guideline of where to cut. Open the quilt up and cut along the pinned line. Refold the quilt, this time bringing the two sides to the middle. Check for accuracy, pinning a guideline for cutting as needed. Open the quilt again, and cut along the pinned line.

Center — Center

## Fabric Selection

The purpose of a binding is to protect the raw edges of the quilt. The binding is usually the first part of a quilt to wear; so, as with all fabrics in a quilt, be sure to choose good-quality, 100 percent cotton cloth. Using a double thickness of fabric, called French fold binding, will increase the durability of the edge.

Fabric for the binding can be a solid or a print found in the quilt top itself or one that, although not present on the top, complements the design in color and pattern. The binding can be the same fabric all the way around, pieced from just a few different fabrics, or intricately pieced.

A helpful way to audition fabric for the binding is to hang the quilt on the design wall or lay it flat on a clean floor. Slip the potential binding fabric under the quilt, letting a little peek out along the edge. This method approximates the amount of fabric that will show in the binding, giving a good visualization of the particular effect of a fabric. For a pieced binding, you can make a small sample and test it.

The binding can work as a frame around the quilt. To achieve this effect, select a binding that contrasts in value, color, or pattern with the fabric on the outer edges of the quilt. For example, if the outer border of the quilt is royal blue, the binding could be navy. Navy would relate to the blue in the border but would stand out because it is darker than royal blue.

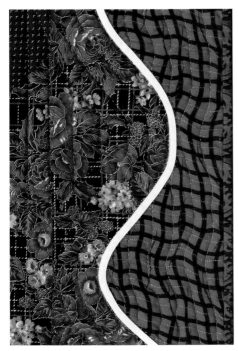

*Six Blonde Ladies.*
Because it's a red fabric similar to the fabric in the outer border, the binding blends into the quilt and does not make a separate design statement. See full quilt on page 4.

*The Gem.*
Although the binding is the same fabric all the way around, it contrasts in color and pattern with the border fabrics. The binding stands out. The fabric is also a stripe, which, when used as bias, creates an exciting finish to this little piece. See full quilt on page 42.

*Conifers Across the Bay.*
The binding was made from the green and orange fabrics used for the trees. Pieced to look like stripes, the design adds a visual rhythm to the outer edge of the finished quilt. Extra inches of green fabric avoid seams at the binding's corners. See full quilt on page 87.

*Wildfire*, Melody Crust, 24″ × 36″ (61 cm × 91.4 cm), machine quilted; private collection.

The binding is pieced so that it changes color as the fabrics in the background change color. This binding finishes the edge but does not call attention to itself, as a contrasting binding would.

## Techniques

Several other methods of finishing a quilt's edge are possible if encasing it in binding is not pleasing on a particular quilt. In each case, the outer edge of the quilt will be the top or backing fabric from the quilt itself. For this reason, none of these edge finishes offers the durability of a separately applied binding. The alternative methods are

- Separately turn the edges of the top and backing under ¼" (0.6 cm), trim away any excess batting, and whipstitch the edges closed.
- Bring the backing fabric to the top, turn under the raw edge, and stitch neatly.
- Bring the top fabric to the back, turn under the raw edge, and stitch neatly.

- Face the edge. Cut two strips of fabric the length of the left and right sides of the quilt and two strips of fabric the length of the top and bottom, plus ½" (1.3 cm). Right sides together, sew one strip down the left side and turn the extra fabric strip to the back. Do the same with the right-hand edge of the quilt. Trim the strips even with the top and bottom edges of the quilt. Right sides together, center the third strip along the top edge and sew. Center and sew the fourth along the bottom. Turn these facing strips to the back. Fold under the raw edges of all four facing strips and whipstitch them to the back of the quilt, squaring up the corners neatly.

The binding can blend with the fabrics in the outer border and not make a separate design statement at all. Blending will occur to the greatest degree when the binding fabric is the same fabric as the outer border fabric. However, similar blending can be achieved by using a fabric that matches the color and value of the outer border fabrics but is not present in the quilt top.

## Finished Width of the Binding

Traditionally, the finished width of binding is ¼" (0.6 cm) to ⅜" (0.95 cm). This size gives a neat, precise edge to the quilt. For design reasons, a much narrower or much wider binding may be applied. The same width of binding will not necessarily complement every quilt.

## Cutting the Binding

Binding is best cut on the bias or on the crosswise grain of the fabric. The lengthwise fibers (parallel to the selvage) have very little stretch. Binding cut on the lengthwise grain will be difficult to apply, and the resulting edge will be stiff.

Fabric cut on the bias or on the crosswise grain is stretchy. This quality makes binding application easier, especially turning corners. Bias binding wears better than crosswise binding, because no threads run parallel to the edge of the quilt; they are at a 45-degree angle to it. For this reason, bias binding may be the best choice for a quilt that will experience heavy use. On the other hand, binding cut on the crosswise grain is more economical. For crosswise binding, just the yardage needed for the binding can be purchased. For bias binding, much more yardage must be purchased and awkward triangles of fabric will be left over.

Some simple arithmetic is all that is needed to determine how wide to cut the binding strips. Assume that the finished width of the binding will be ⅜" (0.95 cm).

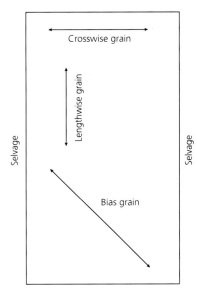

The lengthwise grain runs parallel to the selvages. Crosswise grain is perpendicular to the lengthwise grain and runs selvage to selvage. The bias is at a 45-degree angle to the lengthwise and crosswise grains.

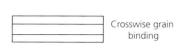

Crosswise grain binding

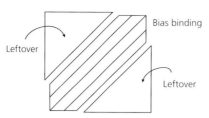

Bias binding

Leftover

Leftover

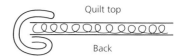

Quilt top

Back

Because strips of binding cut on the crosswise grain parallel a side of the fabric, the exact amount of fabric needed can be purchased. Bias binding is more wasteful of fabric (except that the extra parts can be returned to your fabric cupboard). The strips for bias binding must be cut diagonally out of the central portions of the fabric, leaving unused triangles on either side.

Six is the multiplier because of the way the double-fold binding is applied. On the front, two layers of fabric make up the seam allowance, and two layers fold over to encase the raw edge. Two additional layers cover the edge on the back of the quilt.

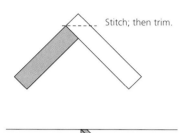

Stitch; then trim.

To seam two lengths of binding together, overlap the diagonally cut ends at a 90-degree angle, right sides together. Adjust so that when sewn with a ¼″ (0.6 cm) seam allowance, the long edges will be straight. Stitch with a ¼″ (0.6 cm) seam. Press open.

1. Multiply ⅜″ (0.95 cm) by 6.
2. Add ¼″ (0.6 cm). The extra width allows for the binding to wrap around the thickness of the batting. If the batting is very thick, more may need to be added. If the batting is very thin, only ⅛″ (0.3 cm) may be necessary. For this example, the cut dimension will be 2½″: ⅜″ × 6 = 2¼″ + ¼″ = 2½″ (6.35 cm: 0.95 cm × 6 = 5.7 cm + 0.6 cm = 6.35 cm).

To find the length of the binding, measure the sides and ends of your quilt. To this sum add about 12″ (30.5 cm) to allow for turning corners.

Seam the lengths together. Press the seams open to reduce bulk. Press the binding down the center, wrong sides together, being careful not to stretch it.

## Applying the Binding

To apply the binding, complete the following steps:

1. Attach the walking foot to your sewing machine or enable the even-feed feature to help the sewing machine feed all layers simultaneously.
2. Loosely pin the pieced binding to the quilt before starting to sew, adjusting as needed so that seams in the binding do not fall at the corners.
3. With the raw edges of the binding aligned with the raw edges of the quilt, begin stitching about 8″ (20.3 cm) from the end of the binding. The seam allowance will be the finished width of the binding. For this example, the seam allowance will be ⅜″ (0.95 cm).

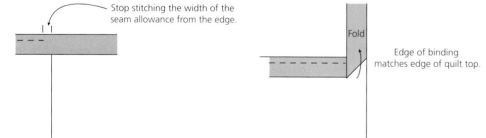

Stop stitching the width of the seam allowance from the edge.

Fold

Edge of binding matches edge of quilt top.

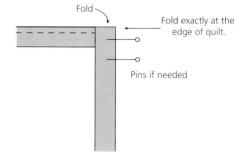

Fold

Fold exactly at the edge of quilt.

Pins if needed

To turn the corner of the binding, stop stitching the width of the seam allowance from the edge. Remove the quilt from under the presser foot, and fold the binding first at a 45-degree angle and then at a 90-degree angle to form the corner. Reposition the quilt to sew the next side with the appropriate seam allowance. This line of stitching should begin with some backstitching to anchor the threads. The 90-degree fold must rest exactly along the edge of the quilt for a perfectly square corner.

4. At the corner, stop stitching the width of the seam allowance from the edge—in this case, ⅜″ (0.95 cm)—and backstitch.

5. Turn the corner.

6. Continue applying the binding until all four corners are sewn. Stop stitching about 12″ (30.5 cm) from the starting point.

7. Backstitch and remove the quilt from under the presser foot.

8. Join the ends of the binding, and finish stitching the binding to the quilt.

The final step in applying the binding is to fold the binding over the raw edge of the quilt and sew by hand with a neat, invisible stitch. When stitching the corners, be sure to distribute the bulk evenly on both sides of the miter. Also, stitch the corner folds closed on the front as well as the back of the quilt.

To join the ends of the binding, follow these steps:

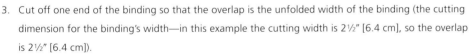

Overlap is cut width of binding. It should always be square.

1. Stop stitching about 12″ (30.5 cm) from the starting point.

2. Lay the quilt flat, and pin the binding in place until it overlaps the unstitched tail at the beginning.

Seam

Trim to ¼″

Finger press seam open.

Stitch

3. Cut off one end of the binding so that the overlap is the unfolded width of the binding (the cutting dimension for the binding's width—in this example the cutting width is 2½″ [6.4 cm], so the overlap is 2½″ [6.4 cm]).

4. Remove the pins and unfold the binding.

5. Lay the unstitched tails right sides together at right angles.

6. Pin along the diagonal stitching line, and check to see if the binding will lie correctly.

7. Make any adjustments; then stitch the seam.

8. Trim the seam allowance to ¼″ (0.6 cm) and finger press open to reduce bulk.

9. Position the binding along the unsewn edge of the quilt, and stitch.

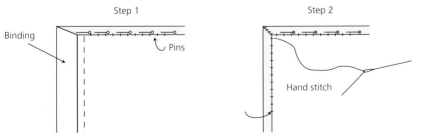

Step 1

Binding

Pins

Step 2

Hand stitch

To distribute the bulk at the corners of the binding, first pin the binding in place along the edge you are approaching. Then sew up to the corner, sew the corner closed front and back, and continue stitching along the new edge.

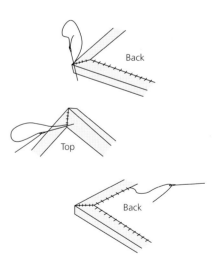

Back

Top

Back

An easy method to stitch front and back folds of the binding corners is to stitch the back fold as you approach the corner. Insert the needle at the corner and bring it out through the fold of the binding corner on the front of the quilt. Stitch this fold closed. Insert the needle at the end of the front fold and bring it out the back. Continue stitching the binding closed along the new edge.

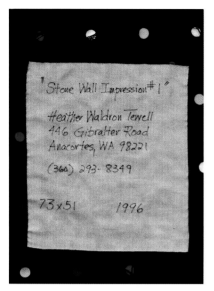

*Stone Wall Impression #1.*

This label was created with the utmost simplicity. A rectangle of plain fabric was first ironed to freezer paper; then the essential information was inked with a permanent-ink pen. See full quilt on page 11.

*Friends & Relations.*

This label, created with a permanent-ink pen on plain fabric, is a straightforward presentation that serves to explain the names on the front of this remembrance quilt. See full quilt on page 16.

# Labels: Plain and Fancy

The label for a quilt is most often sewn to the back. Even when a quilter chooses to sign the front, a label on the back with additional information may be helpful. Some quilters think of labels as functional items providing information and therefore choose a simple, direct method for making them. Others enjoy extending the creative process to their label making and design elaborate productions. Do what works for you, but always label your work.

## *Information on the Label*

At a minimum, the label should include

- name of the maker
- city and state of residence
- year the quilt was completed

Other helpful information would be

- title of the quilt
- dimensions (height by width)
- mailing address
- telephone number
- pattern name, if any
- signature in the quilter's handwriting
- copyright symbol ©
- photo of recipient or maker
- the relationship of the recipient to the quilt maker
- any other historical information about you and your family that would be an interesting addition to this quilt over the years

## *Plain Labels*

The simplest label can be made with some fabric, a permanent-ink pen, and freezer paper. The easiest way to write on fabric is to use freezer paper to stabilize it. The paper temporarily adheres to the fabric pieces when pressed shiny side down using a dry iron at cotton setting. The paper does not damage the fabric, peels off easily, and leaves no residue. Freezer paper is available at grocery stores in the canning supplies section.

To make a plain label, follow these steps:

1. Cut a square of fabric large enough to hold your information. A 6″ (15.2 cm) square is a good size for the minimum information.
2. Cut a square of freezer paper 1″ (2.5 cm) smaller than the fabric. Draw some dark, horizontal lines spaced 1″ (2.5 cm) apart across the freezer paper.
3. Iron the freezer paper to the back of the fabric, shiny side to the fabric.
4. Tape the unit to a window in the daylight or to a light table.

5. Write the information (name, city and state, year completed) on the fabric with a permanent-ink pen, using the lines on the freezer paper to keep the writing straight.
6. Press the edges under ½″ (1.3 cm) all around the label.
7. Remove the freezer paper.
8. Appliqué the label to the back of the quilt.

Another method, nearly as simple, is to use the letters programmed into some sewing machines. Playing around with the lettering on scraps first will help with placement. To use preprogrammed letters, follow these steps:

1. Layer the fabric with tear-away paper, or use an embroidery hoop as for machine embroidery.
2. Program each line of text (name, city and state, year, plus any additional information) into the sewing machine.
3. Stitch with a thread that contrasts with the fabric so that the lettering shows.
4. Remove the paper, using tweezers if necessary.
5. Turn the edges under and appliqué the label to the back of the quilt.

## Fancy Labels

For a fancy label, these supplies are necessary:

- colorfast marking pens in various colors and sizes (thin to thick)
- a calligraphy book or computer with various fonts (styles of lettering)
- freezer paper
- computer paper
- appliqué pattern

Without a computer, start by making a paper pattern for the label. From your idea books or your own inspiration, choose a motif that suits the theme of your label. Trace it onto the paper pattern. To keep the lettering straight, draw horizontal lines on the pattern, avoiding the motif. Then choose a style and size of lettering. Either trace the letters from the calligraphy book or do your own calligraphy using a black permanent-ink pen. These lines will be traced onto the fabric label, so they need to be dark.

A computer is a marvelous tool for making the paper pattern. Select the font style and size from the fonts menu. Play around with placement until the design is pleasing. Remember to save space for your motif if you plan to use one. Print out the label information using black ink, and trace the motif in place.

Once the paper pattern is complete, choose the fabric for the label. Fabric left over from the quilt top makes an excellent coordinated label. A leftover pieced or appliquéd block works well, especially when patches are large enough to contain the lettering.

Cut freezer paper 1″ (2.5 cm) smaller than the size of the finished label, and iron it to the back of the label fabric. The fabric should extend about ½″ (1.3 cm) beyond

*Graciela.*

A coloring-book butterfly inspired this label. The pieces were traced on freezer paper, and the letters were arranged by computer to fit. After inking and heat-setting, the pieces were appliquéd together and then stitched to the quilt. See full quilt on page 6.

*Ping An.*

This font style was selected because it looked Chinese. Using leftover pieces helps unify the back and the front. The thin red strips were cut on the bias so that they could be shaped in circles. See full quilt on page vi.

*Nababeep.*

This appliqué pattern easily became a label. The title and the maker's name were inked on the center, with the address placed on the stem. The slanted letters were done with the computer. See full quilt on page 108.

*Roses Are Red.*

A traditional appliqué pattern was adapted for this label. After inking, the pieces were stitched together before they were sewn to the quilt. Blue embroidery thread outlines the appliquéd shape, separating the label from the busy background fabric. See full quilt on page 57.

the freezer paper. If a leftover block is to be the label, cut freezer paper the size of the patch where the label information will be placed and iron it to the back of the block.

Tape the paper pattern to a bright window or a light table. Position the prepared fabric or block over the pattern, and trace the motif and lettering. Using several colors of permanent-ink pens adds drama to the label.

After inking, place the label fabric side down and press the outer edges under by ½″ (1.3 cm). Heat sets the ink, and the pressed edge provides a guide for stitching. Remove the freezer paper. Appliqué the label to the back of the quilt using an invisible stitch.

An appliqué pattern can be used as the base for a special label. Make the paper template using one of the previously described methods, being sure that the letters are sized to fit the appliqué. Ink the letters onto the fabric. To make attaching the label easier, sew as many of the appliquéd patches together as possible before stitching the label to the back of the quilt.

## Sleeves

A sleeve is a tunnel of fabric applied to the back of a quilt. A rod inserted in the sleeve will firmly support the hanging quilt without causing damage.

### *Fabric for the Sleeve*

The back of a quilt will look best if the fabric for the sleeve coordinates with the backing on the quilt. Quilt backs are seen an amazing number of times during hanging and takedown at shows and at home in everyday use. They, too, should be pleasant to look at.

Some quilters like to construct their sleeves from the same fabric as the binding. Their theory is that the binding of a quilt will wear first. The sleeve can be a source of fabric from which to repair the binding, and a new sleeve can be created.

The sleeve can be made from one continuous length of fabric or it can be pieced. If the sleeve is pieced, press the seam allowances to one side and topstitch so a rod inserted in the pocket will not catch on a seam allowance and rip the fabric.

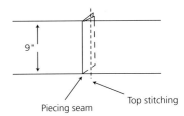

When a sleeve needs to be pieced to get the necessary length, press the seam to one side; then topstitch. This extra step will ensure that the seam allowance will not catch and rip when the rod is inserted.

### *Construction*

The sleeve described will accept a rod 3″ (7.6 cm) to 4″ (10.2 cm) in diameter, the common hanging device for local and national quilt shows. This sleeve will have sufficient fullness so the diameter of the rod will be taken up in the sleeve, allowing the front of the quilt to hang flat.

To construct the sleeve, complete these steps:

1. Cut your chosen fabric 9″ (22.9 cm) wide by the width of the quilt.
2. Fold the sleeve in half lengthwise, wrong sides together, and press lightly.
3. Open the sleeve and bring the long edges, wrong sides together, toward the pressed centerline, holding them 1″ (2.5 cm) away from each other in the middle. This spacing gives the extra fullness necessary to accept a 3″ (7.6 cm) to 4″ (10.2 cm) hanging rod.
4. Press these folds firmly. They become the hand-stitching lines.
5. With wrong sides together and raw edges even, machine stitch the length of the sleeve using a ¼″ (0.6 cm) seam allowance. Backstitch at both ends.
6. Press this seam open using only the point of the iron to avoid pressing over the hand-sewing lines.
7. Fold the short ends under ½″ (1.3 cm); then fold a second time.
8. Machine stitch the hem closed.

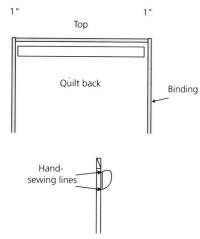

1"          1"

Top

Quilt back

Binding

Hand-sewing lines

Position the sleeve on the back of the quilt so that it is centered left and right. The top of the sleeve should not extend over the binding, and the ends should be about 1" (2.5 cm) inside both sides. Hand stitch along the two firmly pressed folds. The side of the sleeve toward the quilt will lie flat against the quilt; the side of the sleeve away from the quilt will protrude to accept the hanging rod.

## Application

To hand stitch the sleeve to the back, follow these steps:

1. On the back at the top edge of the quilt, center the sleeve with the long seam toward the quilt. When flattened, the sleeve should not overlap the binding along the top edge of the quilt. The sleeve should be about 1" (2.5 cm) inside the left and right sides of the quilt.
2. Pin the sleeve in place along both firmly pressed folds. Some extra fabric should puff away from the quilt. This excess allows for the diameter of the rod.
3. Stitch the sleeve in place using an invisible stitch. Be careful not to stitch through to the front. Reinforce the corners by double stitching for an inch or so on each side. These are points of stress as the rod is inserted and taken out of the pocket.

## Rods

Many shows use a 3" (7.6 cm) or 4" (10.2 cm) pipe as the hanging rod. For home or gallery use, wood laths work well and are available at the lumberyard. Laths come in various widths and thicknesses. A good average size is 2" (5.1 cm) wide by ⅜" (0.95 cm) thick. Cut the lath 1" (2.5 cm) shorter than the width of the quilt so it will not show. Drill a small hole near the top edge at each end. The hole will accept a nail, screw, or line for hanging.

## In Review

Sewing on an attractive binding completes the design of your quilt. Taking time to sew on a label allows you to be credited for your work. Providing a sleeve for hanging ensures that your quilt will not be harmed while on display for all to enjoy. The exercises that follow will help you perfect your skills.

1. Cut crosswise grain and bias binding strips. Bind the samples you made in the exercise in Chapter Six. Evaluate which binding was the easiest to apply and produced the most successful-looking binding.
2. Iron a freezer paper square to a piece of fabric. Practice inking your name and the date. Include the name of your quilt, and apply the new label to the back of the quilt.
3. Return to your study of quilts in books, magazines, and photographs, paying particular attention to each binding. Is it one color? Multicolored? Striped? What makes each a good (or not so good) choice for the quilt?

This sketch uses the shape-and-background-filler approach, with the appliquéd patches and square piecing as the shapes. The design suggests repeating curves where there are curves—around the flowers and the center circle—and using straight lines in various ways as complementary additions. The double parallel lines behind the appliquéd flowers change direction behind each block to repeat the radiating nature of the flowers' placement and unite the four center blocks into one center medallion. For variety, double lines become single, more widely spaced parallel lines over the inner triangles and white border. The basket weave suggested for the white border uses diagonal lines in both directions, just as lines change direction behind the flowers. To maintain even density, a single line of stitching is suggested for the narrow, colored border. This quilting design is big and bold like the quilt top.

The marking of this design can easily be done with a silver pencil before the quilt is basted. The quilt is not large, so the lines should remain visible for the entire quilting process. Another approach is to mark the major lines and fill in the rest later. Only one of the double parallel lines behind the appliquéd flower needs to be marked; the other can be eyeballed or stitched with a sewing guide if you're using the machine. In the basket weave, the triangles can be marked before basting. The filler parallel lines can be marked for hand quilting just before stitching or machine stitched using a sewing guide.

The funky style of this quilt comes from the stylized blossoms, leaves, and flowerpots as well as from the fact that the shapes are large in relation to the size of the quilt. The quilting needed to reflect this bold character.

Considering the entire quilt as the design unit, an overall pattern can be used; or the four large blocks and successive borders can be seen as independent elements, allowing individualized quilting designs to be created.

The repetitive nature of an overall pattern will not add much interest to the quilt surface, but crisp simplicity can be striking and may work well here. A large-scale grid (something like 2″ [5.1 cm]) will work, but a large-scale hanging-diamonds pattern might repeat the funky character better. Hanging diamonds has the feeling of an asymmetrical design, more in keeping with the offbeat quilt top. In order to avoid stitching across the flowers, leaves, and flowerpots with white thread (assuming white would be chosen to match the background fabric), these elements can be skipped when you're stitching the diamonds. These shapes can be quilted in matching thread with some simple lines inside the shapes.

If this quilt will be a baby quilt and not a wall hanging, batting choice will be determined by the density of the quilting lines. A quilt that will be washed and used needs to be made with a batting that will withstand the fiber migration caused by handling. Also, with the bright white background fabric, a white batting will be necessary to avoid shadow-through.

*(continues)*

This sketch goes a bit overboard in playing on the funky nature of the quilt top. However, whether stitched by hand or machine, the actual stitched lines will be much less obvious than these pencil ones. The design can be fun and lighthearted—just what is called for on this top.

Where the previous sketch emphasized lines changing direction, this sketch builds on circles. Starting with a circle around the flower heads, lines of echo quilting are suggested, making ever larger rings until they run into each other or bump into the border. The circles can be perfectly precise but may be more in keeping with the whimsical character if they are childlike and crudely drawn instead. Continuing the idea of concentric rings, circles and half circles fill the borders. The half circles in the outer border are alternated with a wedge shape repeated from the flower petals. The corner resolution is purposefully irregular to emphasize the informal character. An alternative is to redraw the half circles so they come out more evenly at the corners. A simple line maintains the stitching density across the colored strip.

A somewhat more restrained treatment of this quilt top pairs wavy lines with straight lines. The lines become more curved and the stitching pattern more complex as the design develops from the middle outward. This placement fills the emptiest places on the quilt top with the most complex stitching and puts the fancy stitching in the plain white borders, where it will show.

The appliquéd blocks are sketched with simple parallel lines to be stitched without regard to the appliquéd elements. To add interest, two blocks use vertical lines and two use horizontal lines. Parallel lines, but this time contrasting curves, are suggested for the triangle border. These lines can be perfectly parallel or they can be imperfect like the sketch. They can also be more curved. Any of these ideas are in keeping with the lighthearted character of the quilt. The colored inner border is shown with a single wavy line, but it might be interesting to make it a straight line down the long sides and change to a wavy line where it will parallel the waves over the triangles.

For the outer borders the wavy lines continue, but this time they cross. Because the outer borders are two different widths, two designs are needed to fill the spaces from seam to outer edge. The corners need not resolve perfectly but can butt together to continue the informal presentation. These designs are variations on a cable and can be easily stitched by hand or machine.

The relatively simple label of an embroidered lollipop reflects the quilt's theme. The quilt's name, makers' names, dimensions, the year, and the place the quilt was completed are inked with many different pens, the same colors as the appliqué.

*Lollipop*, Melody Crust and Heather Waldron Tewell, 35″ × 42″ (88.9 cm × 106.7 cm), machine quilted.

The quilting follows the design used in the right sketch on page 146. The quilting is stitched with white machine-embroidery thread. Being fairly fine, this thread will not appear too thready when quilted over the appliquéd shapes. The candy-striped binding repeats the fabrics used in the appliqué and continues the upbeat feeling of this little quilt out to the edge.

# Bibliography

## Designing the Quilting

Chainey, Barbara. *Quilt It!* Bothell, WA: That Patchwork Place, 1999.

Cleland, Lee. *Quilting Makes the Quilt.* Bothell, WA: That Patchwork Place, 1994.

Cory, Pepper. *Mastering Quilt Marking.* Lafayette, CA: C & T Publishing, 1999.

Marston, Gwen, and Joe Cunningham. *Quilting with Style: Principles for Great Pattern Design.* Paducah, KY: American Quilter's Society, 1994.

## Resources for Quilting Ideas

Dairy Barn Southeastern Cultural Arts Center and Lark Books. *The Best in Contemporary Quilts.* Asheville, NC: Lark Books, 1999.

Miller, Phyllis D. *Encyclopedia of Designs for Quilting.* Paducah, KY: American Quilter's Society, 1996.

Osler, Dorothy. *Traditional British Quilts.* London: B. T. Batsford Ltd., 1987.

Quilt San Diego, Stevii Thompson Graves, ed. *Visions: Quilt Expressions.* Nashville, TN: Rutledge Hill Press, 1998.

Rae, Janet. *The Quilts of the British Isles.* New York: E. P. Dutton, 1987.

Smith, Kerry I., ed. *Fine Art Quilts: Work by Artists of the Contemporary QuiltArt Association.* Bothell, WA: Fiber Studio Press, 1997.

## Hand Quilting

Kimball, Jeana. *Loving Stitches: A Guide to Fine Hand Quilting.* Bothell, WA: That Patchwork Place, 1993.

McElroy, Roxanne. *That Perfect Stitch: The Secrets of Fine Hand Quilting.* Lincolnwood, IL: The Quilt Digest Press, 1998.

Rodale Quilt Book Editors. *Flawless Hand Quilting.* Emmaus, PA: Rodale Press, Inc., 1999.

Simms, Ami. *How to Improve Your Quilting Stitch.* Flint, MI: Mallery Press, 1987.

## Machine Quilting

Hargrave, Harriet. *Heirloom Machine Quilting.* Lafayette, CA: C & T Publishing, 1990.

Noble, Maurine. *Machine Quilting Made Easy.* Bothell, WA: That Patchwork Place, 1994.

Noble, Maurine, and Elizabeth Hendricks. *Machine Quilting with Decorative Threads.* Bothell, WA: That Patchwork Place, 1998.